Problem-Solving Today

Problem-Solving Today

Standards for New Leaders
in a Changing Environment

Louis J. Pepe

Published in partnership with the Association of School
Business Officials International (ASBO)

ROWMAN & LITTLEFIELD
Lanham • Boulder • New York • London

Published in partnership with the Association of School Business Officials
International (ASBO)

Published by Rowman & Littlefield
An imprint of The Rowman & Littlefield Publishing Group, Inc.
4501 Forbes Boulevard, Suite 200, Lanham, Maryland 20706
www.rowman.com

6 Tinworth Street, London SE11 5AL, United Kingdom

British Library Cataloguing in Publication Information Available

Library of Congress Cataloging-in-Publication Data
Names: Pepe, Louis J., author.
Title: Problem-solving today : standards for new leaders in a changing environment /
    Louis J. Pepe.
Description: Lanham : Rowman & Littlefield, [2021] | Includes bibliographical
    references. | Summary: "This book is meant to provide a glimpse into differing
    facets of organizational management that allows for continued success through
    refinement of skills promoting operational awareness in today's rapidly evolving
    world of business"—Provided by publisher.
Identifiers: LCCN 2020048594 (print) | LCCN 2020048595 (ebook) |
    ISBN 9781475854510 (cloth) | ISBN 9781475854527 (paperback) |
    ISBN 9781475854534 (epub)
Subjects: LCSH: Problem solving. | Leadership. | Success in business.
Classification: LCC HD30.29 .P47 2021 (print) | LCC HD30.29 (ebook) |
    DDC 658.4/03—dc23
LC record available at https://lccn.loc.gov/2020048594
LC ebook record available at https://lccn.loc.gov/2020048595

This book is dedicated to my daughter Megan who represents the best of today's new leaders who possess not only problem-solving skills but the imagination, creativity, and instincts needed to apply solutions that work. I have watched her transform from an inquisitive adolescent into a highly sought after and respected administrator adept at problem-solving with wisdom beyond her years. Much of her success has come from her ability to comprehend the challenges facing the organizations she has been a part of, by understanding the landscape in which we operate today as leaders in the business of education. She has taken the lessons of hard work and determination and applied them in a way that has led to success at an early age. I continue to learn and benefit from her clarity, candor, and awareness of people and the challenges we face every day. She brings a fresh perspective to our conversations and emanates creativity, inspiration, and sound judgment for which I am blessed to have in my network as a colleague and friend.

My inspiration is drawn from iconic leaders in history who met problems head on with solutions that changed the world they lived in and continue to impact the world we live in, Fredrick Douglas and Winston Churchill, and influential authors, Malcom Gladwell and Simon Sinek along with contemporaries who continue to impart wisdom, knowledge and mentorship—special among them—Oregon Association of School Business Officials Executive Director, and Past President, ASBO International 2009, Angela Peterman, RSBS, SFO.

Contents

Contents

Foreword

Who has never faced a problem? Each of us daily faces issues, problems, and quandaries that require solutions that work.

Many times, we realize our conundrum—that the path is unclear. Other times we don't. However, be assured that we all have problems now and will have new ones in the future, as surely as the sun will rise.

As a result, you can never have too much assistance in coping with problems.

Not the glib sort of solutions, like, "Go ask your buddy." Not the superficial assistance like, "You get what you pay for." But, rather, assistance that comes from a seasoned professional, who has a track record of patience and effective counsel in a myriad of situations. Lou Pepe, a veteran crusader against the ambiguous and the seemingly insurmountable challenges that face us daily, dispassionately breaks down the various components in any knotty decision, and with clear, lucid logic, helps lead a clear path forward.

Will the advice always be guaranteed to be right? Of course not, but it will be advice that carefully balances the competing considerations, asks the right questions, illuminates the issues that need further research. What any advice seeker really wants is an approach that carefully balances the risks, the rewards, and carefully weighs the two. That's precisely what this book delivers!

Who am I and why am I writing this foreword to Lou Pepe's third book? My name is David Dietze, and I have had the distinct privilege of working with Lou over many years, in my role as a board member for one of the top-performing school districts in the nation, where Lou served and serves as superintendent of finance for the district. I was most fortunate to get the board appointment, bringing to bear my many years' experience as a corporate attorney, followed by founding, growing, and ultimately selling my wealth management practice to a publicly traded financial institution. Along the way, our firm was recognized as one of the premier wealth managers in the country, by such illustrious luminaries as CNBC and Bloomberg. We built our practice from scratch, ultimately managing hundreds of millions for high-net-worth families and nonprofits. Along the way we became the go-to source for financial insight, interviews, and quotes by *The Wall Street Journal*, *New York Times*, *Los Angeles Times*, Fox, CNN, CNBC, Bloomberg, and a host of others.

Why Lou Pepe? Truth be told, during my over six years working with Lou I became the biggest fan of his analytical style, his diverse range of experience, his negotiating acumen, indeed his problem-solving skills. No wonder that he has parlayed his military experience, private sector work, his tireless advocacy for his community as a council member, his decades of experience in making transparent the opaque world of education finance into becoming one of the deans of school finance. He has taken the time to write two other works, effectively sharing his lifelong experience in leadership, problem-solving, skilled negotiations, and patient strategy, for which I was honored to review and endorse. So, I jumped at the chance to get an advance look at his this third work, indeed a testament to his problem-solving acumen. I felt inspired to share with his readers a foreword, a prefatory analysis of the insightful approaches to basically analyzing a situation, strategically weighing the options, and coming up with the best path to take.

Let's examine the treasure of insights, thirty plus years of experience, and practical strategies that await the reader. Lou has craftily segmented his work into three parts: In part 1, the need for problem-solving is made clear. The fact is, everyone sooner or later will have an issue, a conundrum, and so I can't think of anyone who won't benefit from this careful examination of the importance of problem-solving.

Indeed, that's the very name of the first chapter, where Lou causes us to think about what problems are and why resolution is critical. Chapter 2 breaks down the problem at hand, helping us focus on each essential step that can help us analyze the situation. We are challenged to think critically as to the what and the why of a problem. You'll enjoy the application of the principles to recent well-known business crises.

Chapter 3 explores what factors—both internal and external—affect the problem-solving process. Lou always validates his theories by applying them in the context of a famous intractable crisis, in this chapter the Iran hostage crisis.

Humans distinguish themselves by their well-developed frontal cortex. Lou in chapter 4 challenges us to leverage those capabilities to slay the problem at hand—objectivity is required, not an emotional knee-jerk response. As usual, Lou brings this to life by illustrating with a real-world example from his long career as a business administrator from a well-known school system.

Part 2 of Lou's work brings the reader into thinking intentionally on planning's value. Lou does a deep dive into the difference between superficial knowledge of, say, an organization and really understanding the "skinny" of its inner workings and culture. While it seems obvious, his use of examples and insights from his long and varied career is what brings it to life.

Lou also explores the power of networking—drawing from his real-world experiences growing up in a large extended New Jersey family to navigating his objectives through various communities and associations. You won't hear the term "networking" and have the same appreciation for it after you immerse yourself in Lou's exploration of the topic. Lou continues by focusing on the reality that you can't solve all problems on your own. You need to collaborate, and to get the most value of those associations you must vest your team with real control, effectively communicated by the term "empowerment."

Part 3 synthesizes the outstanding precepts and examples of the first two parts to address actually executing on your analysis: "Implementing Solutions." Of critical importance, Lou lays bare what it takes to be an effective communicator, bringing his years of experience to this topic. I particularly enjoyed the chapter on courage—following the precepts in the first part of the book will help you to develop an intelligent solution, but that solution may be unpopular and not win you friends. This chapter helps you look deep down to develop the willingness to do what's right, what your reason and planning lead you to. Lou's dissection of Johnson & Johnson's Tylenol crisis is brilliant. The capstone, the final chapter, reminds us that change and new problems are inevitable—develop a system, guideposts, to peer out into the future to get prepared for new problems.

In sum, Lou Pepe has done us a great favor by distilling his experience, his wisdom, his thoughts on a topic most don't think about as much as we should, problem-solving. No matter your occupation, your passion, your goals, take advantage of this book to improve your insight into how to prepare for, solve, communicate on, and be courageous in the face of problems.

David G. Dietze, JD, CFA, CFP
President and CIS of Point View Wealth Management, Inc.
Frequent guest on CNBC, Fox, Bloomberg, CNN, and regularly
quoted in *Barron's*, *Wall Street Journal*, and *Los Angeles Times*

Preface

People who are unable to motivate themselves must be content with mediocrity, no matter how impressive their other talents.

—Andrew Carnegie

Reality Based Leadership (RBL) © A conceptual framework of common sense!

—Louis J. Pepe, CFO, MBA, RSBA, SFO

The RBL series is written based on my thirty years of management experience in building, managing, and leading teams to achieve desired outcomes while completing tasks, implementing strategies, and accomplishing goals. This is necessary in any organization to accomplish the ultimate objective—the mission.

Each book is meant to provide a glimpse into differing facets of organizational management that allows for continued success through refinement of skills promoting operational awareness in today's rapidly evolving world of business.

Problem-solving is essential to success and goal attainment in any industry, company, organization, or team. Challenges are why we exist as managers and leaders. It is what allows for the "value add" that each of us possess to showcase talents and employ problem-solving skills in providing solutions that work. Solving the problems we face as individuals, leaders, and managers is what allows us to forge ahead amidst constant challenges and setbacks that would otherwise short-circuit or end our careers and the prosperity of the companies, stakeholders, and organizations that count on us.

The Germans have a saying that goes something like this: "It's never eaten as hot as it's cooked" (proverbial meaning: Things are never as bad as they seem). Instead we let these hot items cool before attempting to eat them as not to get burned. That advice is especially on point for problems when considering their magnitude and our reaction to them. The extra time

"Es wird nichts so heiß gegessen, wie es gekocht wird."

afforded to waiting allows one to absorb the impact and think clearly in understanding the cause and effect of the problem at hand while considering the available options or begin generating better solutions to effectively solve. Problem-solving is a talent, skill, and requirement needed to stay ahead of difficulties, challenges, and issues that confront each of us from time to time in our professional endeavors. The adage "Hast makes waste" is as true today as it was the first time I heard it from my father over forty years ago.

Like so many phrases I have taken from my German wife who likewise learned these timeless principles from her father, it underscores the importance of patience prior to diving in to apply a "fix" that could actually exacerbate an already tenuous situation only to create new or bigger issues. The saying is steeped in soundness and—if followed—allows for real solutions that not only solve but often improve situations and leave us with the added benefit of experience, knowledge, and wisdom.

This common saying encourages individuals to approach problem-solving with an open and creative mind by expanding options through data analysis, proven techniques, imagination, and innovation to not only solve but also improve our outcomes. This is especially true of achieving operational gains and fostering open environments that reward questioning the status quo. By encouraging a growth mindset we encourage our people to strive to do better and achieve more by allowing them to take risks, fail, and learn. The results are often extraordinary discoveries that catapult us beyond our competition and mark our leaders as visionaries who are unafraid to lead.

The subject matter in this book is not just advice for the reader; it is tried and true evidence of success and failure experienced by many who value the importance of brainstorming, collaboration, and resilience in tackling today's problems in preparation of learning and improving how we meet the challenges of tomorrow.

Over a thirty-plus-year career in leadership, collaboration, and problem-solving, this is something that I have worked to master and continue to seek improvements whenever and wherever possible. That's how important it is and it requires a deep appreciation for the value of creative problem-solving.

Life is a series of experiences, each one of which makes us bigger, even though sometimes it is hard to realize this. For the world was built to develop character, and we must learn that the setbacks and grieves which we endure help us in our marching onward.

—Henry Ford

I have found the best problem solvers are those who lack the fear of failing but instead view it as mere attempts to solve.

Louis J. Pepe
Lincoln Park, New Jersey
2020

Acknowledgments

I would like to start by thanking my board members past and present who have given me the many opportunities over the years to apply my problem-solving skills in ways that allowed me to grow as a professional and master the skills I have shared in this book.

Likewise, I remain indebted to NJSBA, New Jersey School Boards; NJASBO, New Jersey Association of School Business Officials; AASA, the School Superintendents Association; and ASBO, the Association of School Business Official International for the many opportunities to gain a deeper appreciation of the skills necessary to master our changing environments and ultimately succeed in providing quality leadership for the organizations, stakeholders, and students we serve.

I'm forever indebted to Pat George for putting me in touch with Tom Koerner at Rowman & Littlefield Publishers, Inc., and Jeff McCausland, founder and CEO of Diamond6 Leadership and Strategy, LLC, for guiding me on the book proposal process. It is because of their efforts and encouragement that I have a legacy to pass on to my colleagues and leaders in the many fields of management.

Part 1

THE NEED FOR PROBLEM-SOLVING

Chapter 1

The Importance of Problem-Solving Skills (Beyond IQ)

Problem solvers have been in demand since the beginning of time. They are the people in any successful organization that exhibit the skills necessary to look beyond the problems at hand in order to come up with solutions that work. More important, they deliver the plans that bring order to chaos and remove uncertainty from the needed actions to move forward toward such solutions. We often refer to "the smartest person in the room"; however, when it comes to solving problems, you don't have to be the smartest person in the room to solve the problem—just the most creative, grounded, and fearless and therefore the most valuable person (MVP) in the room.

At Google, the MVP is not the candidate with the highest GPA who necessarily lands the job, but the individual with general cognitive ability or learning ability. "It's the ability to process on the fly. It's the ability to pull together disparate bits of information. It is the No. 1 thing they look for in the hiring process."[1] Second is leadership.

Problem-solving is all about finding solutions to mitigate situations that are unwelcomed or harmful. These situations need to be dealt with and overcome before the harm turns into damage or even tragedy. The longer we delay, the deeper the damage.

Effective problem-solving generates solutions that not only solve our problems but also serve to improve our circumstances, which in turn, enrich our lives. Regardless of their size or degree of impact, problems can harm our operations, our people, and ultimately our ability to carry out our mission. Finding the right solutions that work in addressing these problems is a vital component of leadership. When properly applied, problem-solving not only addresses the issues we face but also fosters success in a way that protects our investments and guarantees our future.

In order to be successful, we need goals; without goals, our plans will never take shape or at least prove ineffective over time. Without goals, we are lost and have no direction. This concept was presented in the second book in this series, *Planning for Success—Strategies That Enhance the Process of Goal Attainment*.

In his book *Beyond IQ: Scientific Tools for Training Problem Solving, Intuition, Emotional Intelligence, Creativity, and More*,[2] Garth Sundem makes the argument, "Sure, having a high IQ is great. But surprisingly, science shows that mental abilities not captured in IQ tests can have the most impact in the real world—attributes like creativity, willpower, emotional intelligence, and intuition."[3]

It is these attributes that lend themselves to acquiring a "growth mindset"—a flexible way of confronting issues to seek solutions that turn out better solutions and thus better more positive outcomes. It is what makes us stretch, learn, and grow. That growth manifests itself over time in real change that tests our processes—action steps that we take in order to achieve a particular end. It accesses the brain's cognitive ability—our mental capability to reason, plan, and think in abstract terms while dealing with complex ideas through comprehension and learning from our past experiences. This is where experiential learning is applied in a free-thinking way that breaks the mold of a limited or fixed mindset associated with the deadly phrase—"That's the way we always did it," which now comes complete with its acronym, "TTWWADI."

> Individuals who believe their talents can be developed (through hard work, good strategies, and input from others) have a growth mindset. They tend to achieve more than those with a more fixed mindset (those who believe their talents are innate gifts). This is because they worry less about looking smart and they put more energy into learning. When entire companies embrace a growth mindset, their employees report feeling far more empowered and committed; they also receive far greater organizational support for collaboration and innovation. In contrast, people at primarily fixed-mindset companies report more of only one thing: cheating and deception among employees, presumably to gain an advantage in the talent race.[4]

Without growth, companies die; first, they stall then they wither until they become irrelevant, broke, and eventually dissolve; The same is true of organizations; when we learn, we grow—as a result of that growth we are able to solve the problems we encounter. With continued growth, we are able to reach new heights and take on larger goals that without such growth would not be possible.

Some people confuse *growth* with *expansion*—they are not the same. While expansion is the act or process of expanding,[5] simply becoming larger does nothing to aid in the process of problem-solving; whereas, growth is an increase in size, number, value, or strength,[6] elements invaluable in the process.

A quick case to illustrate the point:

* Crumbs Bake Shop, Inc.

Crumbs Bake Shop, Inc. CRMBQ Stock Price reported on Nasdaq

CRMBQ—NASDAQ

As reported by *The Wall Street Journal*, Crumbs Bake Shop was once the biggest cupcake vendor in the world.[7] Headquartered in New York City, the bakery chain was founded in 2003 as a small mom-and-pop-style bakery on the Upper West Side of Manhattan by Mia and Jason Bauer. The company expanded to seventy-nine locations in nine states (New York, Illinois, Virginia, Connecticut, New Hampshire, Massachusetts, New Jersey, Rhode Island, and California) and Washington, DC.[8]

"Listed as one of Inc.'s fastest-growing companies, the cupcake chain expanded to many different cities, with dozens of stores, but the growth was not sustainable."[9]

By November 2, 2011, the company's stock price on Nasdaq traded at a high of $5.69 per share with 11,298 shares exchanged between buyers and sellers. It closed that day at $5.31 a share; by June 30, 2014, it was all over as it closed at .11 cents a share following the news that it was to be delisted by Nasdaq the next day.

As described above in the comparison of growth versus expansion, it lacked the elements of growth necessary to solve the problems associated with their expansion. The company was experiencing declining sales, increased competition, higher real estate costs, and waning consumer interest. Despite these problems, they continued to press for expansion, which gave off an outward appearance of growth, health, and prosperity. "In mid-2011, its same-store sales started declining just as the company was orchestrating a massive expansion. Crumbs was forced to begin closing stores, putting its expansion plans on hold."[10]

While many bakers believe there's something about achieving perfection in something as delicate as a cupcake, Crumbs' expansion was covering up the real problems they faced with too much frosting, in this case, the number of stores popping up all over, they were forced to close most of their locations by the time they declared bankruptcy in 2014.

Authors and bloggers alike have been quoting the work of Carol Dweck for the past decade since the release of her groundbreaking book *Mindset: The New Psychology of Success* (2007). Dweck, a renowned Stanford University psychologist, coined the terms *fixed mindset* and *growth mindset* to describe the underlying beliefs people have about learning and intelligence. It has become a strategy for problem-solving by teachers throughout the world and employed in classrooms everywhere.

A key concept of the growth mindset described by Dweck refers to "The Power of Yet," which she covered in a highly successful TED talk in Sweden in 2014. Her TED talk[11] has since received more than 10 million views. The concept is straightforward and apt in the discussion of problem-solving as it applies to anyone wishing to succeed and take on greater challenges.

Dweck illustrates the point by sharing a story about a group of high school students in a Chicago school district who received a grade of "Not Yet" for failing to meet the state requirements for graduation. The power given by those two tiny words had a massive impact as they realized success was still available to them—they still had a chance of reaching their goal.

Her work regarding the "growth mindset" puts forward the notion that we can grow our brain's capacity to learn and to solve problems. In her TED talk, she described two ways to address a problem that is slightly too hard for one to solve. One can either quit (fixed mindset) or keep trying and applying the learned knowledge to solve (growth mindset). The power is in the message of "not yet" as those possessing a *growth mindset* have the ability to acknowledge that although they may not be able to solve yet, they have the ability to learn and grow their problem-solving skills to come back to the problem later and conquer it by solving.

While she speaks of student progress in the TED talk, the concepts regarding the growth mindset are applicable to any leader confronted by any problem that seems just beyond their grasp. A growth mindset is what it takes to continue to learn, attempt, fail, and try again until we master the problem by applying what we have learned from those failures. Realizing with each failure that the struggle isn't over and that success is still possible—just not reached, not yet.

That is how organizations survive the challenges they face by having the right people in the right places within the right mindset to solve the problems they face and learning from the process to quicken their problem-solving skills as new challenges emerge. This concept applies to any company or organization and any leader or individual willing to stretch themselves in the pursuit of the goal of success in problem-solving.

Those who quit often see failed attempts as a failure. That is wrong and shortsighted. Failure, taken at face value, equals defeat. Once accepted, it serves to remind us that we have failed and given enough failures leads to a sense of hopelessness and inferiority that breeds lack of confidence and feelings of inadequacy. That is counterproductive and harmful to any attempts for future success. Instead, our failures should be viewed as attempts to solve that simply did not work or achieve the desired results we seek or at least not yet. A growth mindset allows us to learn from our mistakes or failed attempts and translate those attempts into learned knowledge of what doesn't work as we continue to employ alternative actions that eventually breakthrough into discoveries—that lead to success. That is what makes inventors and scientists successful in achieving results that benefit society in ways we could never imagine. Some of the greatest inventions are great because they are practical and allow us to deal with challenges in a way that improves our experiences.

Let's look at a simple exercise in "trial and error"—the .99 cent O-ring. Things always break down at the most inopportune times—that's what happens and that is exactly what happened with my one-year-old Cub Cadet snowblower as a storm had just delivered about six inches of snow this past December. Having set idle in the garage for about ten months, the efforts to start it were in vain. Neither the pull start nor electronic start would turn the engine over and I was left to the reluctant task of shoveling the driveway.

After looking for the manual to work through the troubleshooting guide and watching a number of YouTube videos, I was left with the unavoidable task of removing the carburetor fuel bowl to drain the "bad gas" and clean out the carburetor. Once I removed the bowl, the fuel bowl O-ring designed to create an airtight seal came out with the bowl. Having learned from the videos of *successful do it your selfers*, I replaced the O-ring, blew out the carburetor, and put it all back together in about twenty minutes. I then proceeded to put new gas in and pulled the cord . . . it started like a champ. I ran it for a bit to ensure it was good, going through a few shutdowns and restarts then parked back in the garage—mission accomplished! I then proceeded to walk around the house chanting, "Yes, I have made fire!" . . . taking a page from Tom Hanks in the movie *Cast Away* to impress my wife and celebrate my victory. That lasted about an hour when she went downstairs and came up telling me that she smelled gas. I went into the garage only to discover I now had a new problem. Gas was leaking from the bowl where I had just finished my small engine repair—back to the drawing board. At this point, the carburetor was flooded and the bowl was leaking heavier as I tipped the blower back to move it.

Every time I went through the process of trying to reseat the O-ring and reassemble the carburetor, the bowl leaked. It wasn't working. After attempt number seven or eight, I applied Einstein's theory of insanity defined as trying the same thing over and over expecting a different result. What I learned was every time I took the bowl off and attempted to reseat the O-ring and put the bowl back in place, it continued to leak. I also learned that I needed help, so I elicited the help of my neighbor who has mad mechanical skills and tools that span two sheds and a garage.

He tried the same process of reseating the O-ring and reassembling the bowl about five more times and then it hit us. Although we knew what the problem was, we had to change our approach in order to solve. What we learned was no matter how many times we tried to reseat the O-ring, it was no longer viable and we needed a new one. Of course, we could not locate a replacement ring that fit the grove properly to prevent the gas from breaching the seal. They were either slightly too big, too small, too fat, or too thin. Further complicating the issue was the engine on the blower was manufactured in China and no area dealer carried the individual parts needed, in this case the O-ring. In order to get a replacement, we would have to order a completely new carburetor and that was not going to happen—we had a $1,000 snowblower that was held up by a .99 cent part.

Finally, days later after we received a replacement O-ring we ordered online, we figured we had it licked and we were about ten minutes away from a permanent fix. Through our many previous attempts to solve, we learned how to access the carburetor easier and faster and had become extremely proficient at removing the wheel, the guard, and the bowl quicker cutting the total time in half. It still leaked—we were defeated or so you would think. That's when we went off-script, threw away the manual, and made our own O-ring by cutting a slightly larger, slightly thicker O-ring we purchased at the local hardware store for .99 cents and sized it to fit into the grove in the bowl. We tightened it up and crossed our fingers—it worked! Months later, it is still holding without leaking and the blower is fully functional.

While the O-ring problem example, in this case, was on a small scale with limited impact other than having to return to the shovel during the downtime experienced with fixing the problem, it demonstrates the importance of a growth mindset in reaching success in arriving at a solution that worked.

Conversely, elements of a fixed mindset contributed to the worst O-ring failure in history claiming the lives of seven astronauts on a cold day in January 1986, known forever as the Challenger Space Shuttle Disaster.

While the O-ring failure in this case, identified as the cause of the explosion, characteristics of a fixed mindset were at work leading up to the ill-conceived launch by NASA. They included an agency that had become more interested in looking smart than accepting the challenges to grow and improve. Specific attributes of a fixed mindset displayed by NASA prior to take off were challenge avoidance, defensiveness, hiding flaws, and ignoring negative feedback expressed by those including Allan McDonald, director of the Space Shuttle Solid Rocket Motor Project for the engineering contractor Morton Thiokol. The 256-page report issued by the Rogers Commission[12] in June of that year stated on page 83 that problems with NASA's organizational culture and decision-making processes had been key contributing factors to the accident.

> In addition to analyzing all available evidence concerning the material causes of the accident on January 28, the Commission examined the chain of decisions that culminated in approval of the launch. It concluded that the decision making process was flawed in several ways.[13]

McDonald was concerned that below-freezing temperatures might impact the integrity of the solid rockets' O-rings. Although he was proven right, his concern was dismissed, despite the fact that the night before, he had refused to sign the launch recommendation over safety concerns.[14] As he fought to draw attention to the real reasons behind the disaster, he experienced retribution by individuals from NASA and his employer, Morton Thiokol, Inc., makers of the Shuttle's solid rocket boosters. McDonald later went on to detail his experiences with the Challenger disaster and its aftermath in his book *Truth, Lies, and O-Rings: Inside the Space Shuttle Challenger Disaster*.

The commission found NASA had violated its own safety rules, reporting the following on page 174 of the report:

> "Operational" should not imply any less commitment to quality or safety, nor a dilution of resources. The attitude should be, "We are going to fly high risk flights this year; every one is going to be a challenge, and every one is going to involve some risk, so we had better be careful in our approach to each."[15]

"Uh-oh," a phrase signifying alarm, dismay, or realization of a difficulty, was the last words recorded on the transcript[16] of the Challenger crew comments only seventy-three seconds into the flight. They never saw it coming. In just over a minute, the entire crew was in peril.

> After the collapse of its fuel tank, the Challenger itself remained momentarily intact, and actually continued moving upwards. Without its fuel tank and boosters beneath it, however, powerful aerodynamic forces soon pulled the

orbiter apart. The pieces—including the crew cabin—reached an altitude of some 65,000 feet before falling out of the sky into the Atlantic Ocean below. It's likely that the Challenger's crew survived the initial breakup of the shuttle but lost consciousness due to loss of cabin pressure and probably died due to oxygen deficiency pretty quickly. But the cabin hit the water's surface (at more than 200 mph) a full 2 minutes and 45 seconds after the shuttle broke apart, and it's unknown whether any of the crew could have regained consciousness in the final few seconds of the fall.[17]

As a result of the disaster, NASA took a thirty-two-month hiatus in the shuttle program.

What we can learn from this tragic event in our history is that a growth mindset could have led to a different outcome, one in which the lives of the astronauts might have been spared and the program could have avoided a costly black eye. NASA managers had known since 1977 that contractor Morton-Thiokol's design of the Single Rocket Boosters (SRBs) contained a potentially catastrophic flaw in the O-rings, but they had failed to address this problem properly.[18] In a Morton Thiokol interoffice memo dated July 31, 1985,[19] six months before the tragedy, from R. M. Boisjoly, Applied Mechanics Division to R. K. Lund, Vice President, Engineering, Boisjoly informs Lund of the following critical concerns regarding the SRM O-ring:

Roger Boisjoily's first attempt after STS 51-B (flight 17) to convince his management of the seriousness of the O-ring erosion problem.[20]

Subject: SRM O-Ring Erosion/Potential Failure Criticality

¶ 1—"This letter is written to **insure that management is fully aware of the seriousness** of the current O-Ring erosion problem in the SRM joints from an engineering standpoint."

¶ 2—"The **mistakenly accepted position** on the joint problem was to fly without fear of failure and run a series of design evaluations **which would ultimately lead to a solution or at least a significant reduction** of the erosion problem."

¶ 3—"If the same scenario should occur in a field joint (and it could) . . . **the result would be a catastrophe of the highest order**—loss of human life."

¶ 4—"An unofficial team (a memo defining the team and its purpose was never published) with leader was formed on 19 July 1985 and was tasked with solving the problem for both the sort and long term. This unofficial team is essentially nonexistent at this time. In my opinion, **the team must be officially given the responsibility and the authority to execute the work that needs to be done** on a non-interference basis (full time assignment until completed)."

The day after the disaster the *New York Times* headline read: THE SHUT-TLE EXPLOSION; REAGAN POSTPONES STATE OF UNION SPEECH. The speech would later go on to be memorialized as one of the best speeches of his presidency ending with the words, "We will never forget them, nor the last time we saw them, this morning, as they prepared for their journey and waved goodbye and 'slipped the surly bonds of earth' to 'touch the face of God.'"

Roger Mark Boisjoly passed away in 2012; he was seventy-four years old. He was a mechanical engineer, fluid dynamicist, and an aerodynamicist—sounds pretty smart. At the time of the disaster, he was forty-seven and if not the smartest person in the room, clearly the MVP in the room as he recognized the problem still existed and needed to be solved. Had the higher ups heeded the concern expressed in Boisjoly's memo, the tragedy could have very well been avoided. The fixed mindset that existed not only prevented them from solving the problem they knew existed, it also created a blind spot that put the entire space program in jeopardy.

Chapter 2

A Step-by-Step Process to Problem-Solving

HOW MANY STEPS ARE NECESSARY TO SOLVE PROBLEMS EFFECTIVELY? IS IT 3, 5, 7, OR MORE?

Six Sigma (6σ),[1] a widely recognized tool has five steps with its own acronym—DMAIC. The steps are: (1) define, (2) measure, (3) analyze, (4) improve, and (5) control. Six Sigma is a set of techniques and tools for process improvement. It was introduced by American engineer Bill Smith while working at Motorola in 1980.[2] It begins with identifying the problem by first defining it—*what is the problem* and second by measurement—*determining the degree or scale*. Next, one proceeds to analyze or study the problem much like puzzle solving—*what are the key elements or issues to be considered* before one can advance to the final steps in order to solve by improving and thus gain control over the issue?

ThinkReliability, a Houston-based consulting firm that focuses on solving problems and improving business processes, advises clients not to complicate it. "Solving problems at work can be confusing. With a variety of different tools, it's common for people in the same company to use different approaches and different terminology. This makes problem solving problematic. It shouldn't be."[3] They recommend a three-step approach—problem, analysis, and solutions.[4]

So what do these processes for problem-solving have in common? They all recognize that the first step to solving any problem begins with defining it.

Each problem is unique and requires answers to multiple questions to get at the root definition—"What is the problem? When did it happen? Where did it happen and what was the total impact to each of the organization's overall goals?"[5] You need to go deep in getting to the root of any problem by requiring quantitative information to fully comprehend any issue. On the surface, issues can appear to be simple and straightforward; however, once we begin to dig deep we often find we are simply seeing the effect(s) and not the cause(s). Think back to the iceberg analogy—some problems like icebergs appear small but over 90 percent of an iceberg's volume (mass) is underwater. By gathering all the facts and data surrounding the issue(s), we begin to get a more complete picture of the problem and therefore now have the ability to properly define it prior to setting out to solve.

In the *analysis step*, the focus is on the *why*—why did the problem occur and begins to isolate the *how*—how did the problem occur. This method is effective in looking at all problems large and small and applicable to any business or industry. It relies on the scientific evidence-based method of cause-and-effect relationships. By studying the reasons (or causes) for the problem then discusses the results (or effects) of the problem. This relationship approach to problem-solving has become a recognized form of essay writing sometimes referred to as reason and result essays. It is a unit of study for National Geographic Learning,[6] which focuses on *transitions* and *connectors* to uncover the answers with guidelines to how to construct cause-effect essays as part of their mission: "To bring the world to the classroom and the classroom to life."

The basic premise here is that you cannot solve for what you do not understand. That is how individuals and companies get into trouble by rushing to solve and thus causing bigger issues or moving their organizations or companies further from the mark, or just as bad—doing nothing that guarantees their failure in solving the problem.

Doing nothing will get you nowhere—doing nothing may end your career or your business, or at the very least inflict damage that goes deep, resulting in bad press, loss of confidence, and even loss of value, reflected in a falling stock price per share. While the premise is basic, many individuals and companies fall victim to the plight. Here are a few recent examples that appeared in a January 3, 2018, Forbes article, *10 Major Corporate Blunders That Wouldn't Have Happened If Companies Listened to Their Employees*:

Equifax: In September of 2017, Equifax announced a data breach that exposed the personal information of 147 million people.[7]

"Months before the credit company's data breach that compromised the personal data of 145 million Americans, a security researcher warned the company that it was vulnerable to a large-scale attack. The researcher scanned servers and public-facing websites and discovered customer personal information was easily accessible. Equifax didn't take any action, however, until after the hack took place."[8]

Wells Fargo: On September 8, 2016, federal regulators said Wells Fargo (WFC) employees secretly created millions of unauthorized bank and credit card accounts—without their customers knowing it—since 2011.[9]

"The phony accounts earned the bank unwarranted fees and allowed Wells Fargo employees to boost their sales figures and make more money.

Wells Fargo came under fire for widespread fraudulent accounts in 2016, but an employee tried to alert the CEO of the issue in 2007. The now-former employee was transferred after warning supervisors about unethical behavior happening throughout his region and even warned that the illegal sales practices could lead to fraud, lawsuits, and regulatory sanctions, all of which have recently hit the bank."[10]

Samsung: On January 22, 2017—after months of silence following a global recall of its Galaxy Note 7 smartphone in October of 2016—Samsung disclosed its lengthy findings as to what caused the device's batteries to overheat and catch fire.[11]

"In one of the most disastrous product rollouts in recent years, Samsung's Galaxy Note 7 phone started exploding and burning within a few days of its release, leading to massive recalls. The phone was combustible because too many pieces were crammed into the aggressive design. Employees tried to warn Samsung that the design was risky, but the company continued to introduce the product with terrible results."[12]

Addressing the problem, any problem begins with acknowledgment—whether it is a personal problem, a group problem, or an impact problem, which impacts or disrupts either the individual or the group. The above examples are classic cases in *what not to do* during any problem-solving process. Denial has long been held as a major stumbling block to problem-solving as you first need to clear this hurdle before you can ever start thinking about fixes.

When it comes to longevity, regarding businesses or organizations, that fact remains critical to the company's or organization's survival. In order to go the distance—to complete the journey of reaching our goals—we have to recognize the problems confronting us today and those on the horizon before working to solve them. This requires grit, determination, and perseverance.

In 1982, a rock band Survivor built a song around the Rocky IV movie calling it the "Eye of the Tiger."[13] The eye of the tiger signified a will and determination to go the distance and achieve this goal that seemed unobtainable. Rocky had to figure out a way to beat Ivan Drago the Russian "boxing machine" and to do this he needed everyone in his corner. This required an *all hands on deck* approach to mount an adequate response to the challenge he faced. This is the same approach needed to adequately address challenges in our organizations today, when confronted with insurmountable odds—the "big" challenges.

Regardless of the steps utilized to problem solve, a key component remains the strength of the team in implementing solutions. The *solutions step* begins to take form in the generation of options that need to be evaluated and prior to being implemented and effectively executed to obtain the results we seek.

Smart leaders know effective teams need to consist of other leaders, a strong core of competent leaders with the capacity to listen to opposing viewpoints. They need to be able to discuss solutions, examine alternatives, and consider perspectives of others as well as their own. Collaboration does not mean compromising your thoughts, beliefs, and instincts—it means you have the ability to trust your team to validate those beliefs and perhaps improve or uncover the blind spots in your solution to the problem at hand.

Think of a leader you know, work for, or report to and consider how this next paragraph pertains to them and the effects they have on the organizations they lead, both positive and negative:

Ultimately smart leaders work in a collaborative environment of trust and accountability for *decisions made* and *actions taken* to master their internal environments (positive). Without this ability, they perpetuate mediocrity and experience continued failure to achieve their task(s) (negative). When the leaders we work with become true collaborators, they have a better chance of generating positive outcomes versus creating a climate of negativity, distrust, and disenchantment.

Absent clear direction, focus, and guidance, tasks take on Sisyphean feel as they become insurmountable and we become defeated before we start. Sisyphus, the former king in Greek mythology, came to understand this well as he was forced to roll the immense boulder up a hill only to see it roll back down each time. However, separating myth from reality you can bet that those found rolling boulders in your organization will either leave once they realize the fatalism of their task or stop trying.

So how many steps does it take to solve problems effectively? It reminds me of the old commercial, "How many lick to get to the center of tootsie pop?" The answer—it doesn't really matter as long as the makers of the candy got you to attempt to solve and of course purchase their product.

Problem-solving is really more about process than steps; however, that process must include these basic steps:

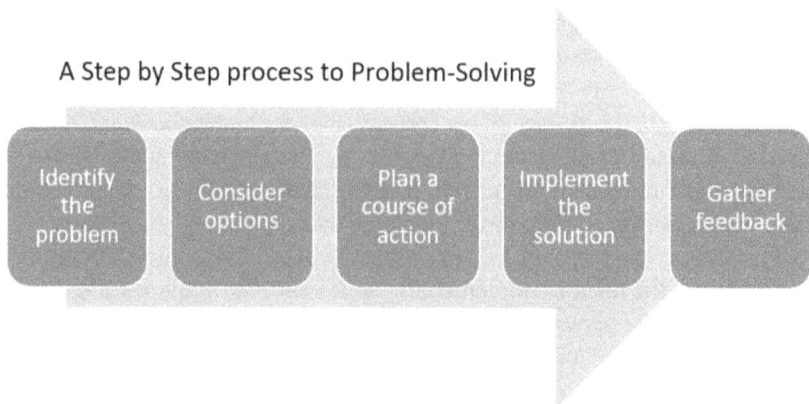

A Step by Step process to Problem-Solving

| Identify the problem | Consider options | Plan a course of action | Implement the solution | Gather feedback |

These steps are key in allowing individuals to quickly and easily become better problem solvers and add to their worth as leaders. In order to master this ability, we need to apply the standards discussed in this book, which center on reason, empowerment, clarity, engagement, collaboration, and research to achieve superior results.

Last, we must consider the role of unity in every aspect of the problem-solving process. Unity is crucial to problem-solving in that we need to achieve unity among our staff, our leaders, and our stakeholders in our approach (1), our response (2), and the desired outcome (3), if we have any hope of attaining success. While we each bring something to the table that makes us unique, it is as a team that we increase our power to problem solve.

We all strive to achieve our goals; however, a shared vision is what helps us unite in our thinking and a shared sense of mission allows us to execute the solution with precision, persistence, and purpose.

So start thinking about all the ways your group or organization may need to find unity to avoid problems and more importantly solve them.

Chapter 3

Factors Affecting Our Approach
to Problem-Solving

Our approach to problem-solving, while rooted in process and structured in steps, is influenced by factors that contribute to the way we deal with issues. Issues come at us daily, most of them generate little to no stress; however, some produce higher levels of stress that can impact our ability to solve them. Clear minds and level heads produce clear direction and instruction that leads to effective actions in addressing problems with solutions as they are targeted. Individuals who allow stress to impact their thinking create situations that are messy, unclear, and ineffective.

Deadlines and other pressures ramp up our stress levels that either increase or decrease our effectiveness in dealing with them, but our stress levels skyrocket when we encounter problems that impede our ability to accomplish our tasks such as the Internet going down right before a big project is due.

Pressures come with the territory in leadership, that's a given; however, good leaders learn to cope with pressure and great leaders convert that pressure into high-octane adrenaline that gives them a boost in finding and employing solutions that work. That's great, but keep in mind that everyone in the organization deals with stress and how they deal with that stress affects their outcomes and ultimately the success or failure of that organization. Stress is a natural reaction that needs to be managed in order to achieve success in any problem-solving scenario. If we fail to manage stress in our workplace, we will never be effective in solving problems.

When it comes to facing problems, each of us reacts in our own unique way that defines our ability to perform under pressure or trademarks our ability to deal with problems. "Some cope with life challenges and stressors better than others . . . the definition, *a reaction to adverse things around you*—because each person perceives and interprets stress/pain uniquely."[1]

Over the years I have witnessed strong competent leaders who performed the assistant role or "Number Two" in an exemplary manner gaining the respect and admiration of all who follow; however, once they are put in the lead role they change and fold under the pressure of being the "Number One."

As leaders, we need to have the ability to focus on the problem at hand in a crisis without allowing emotions to cloud our judgment in a way that blocks our ability to process the situations we encounter. Again depending on the critical nature of the event such as an incident involving health and safety, for example, an emergency in which hazardous conditions are present, we need to be able to take command of the scene and make quick decisions to move individuals out of harm's way until first responders arrive on the scene.

Depending on our role as leaders, we may be tasked with protecting the lives of those in our charge by leading them to safety in the event of an evacuation or ensuring appropriate measure are carried out in a lockdown. Responding to incidents requires that we must be ready, willing, and able to address situations at a moment's notice. This requires training along with the development of coping skills to provide the necessary leadership when it is needed most—in a time of crisis.

Incident command has become a recognized and practiced response for dealing with federal disasters (IS-101.C: Preparing for Federal Disaster Operations) by FEMA.[2] The course is designed for FEMA employees who deploy to domestic incidents. While the course is designed for FEMA workers who deploy to domestic incidents, those they work with at the local level, first responders, Office of Emergency Management (OEM) workers, and community leaders (mayors and council representative), all receive a foundation course (ICS 100, Introduction to the Incident Command System)[3] in order to understand the principles and basic structure of the Incident Command System (ICS).

While many leaders may never serve as first responders or be required to complete emergency management training like the programs offered by FEMA, the techniques, structure, and objectives of these type of training programs help equip any leader with the confidence and skills necessary to deal with critical situations. Those skills are transferable and beneficial to mission critical problem-solving of any kind as they bring structure and focus on how to plan, manage, and coordinate resources for an efficient and effective response to any crisis.

When a crisis hits no matter what type we are facing, it comes at us fast especially in the digital era where news goes viral. Often this pushes leaders to react too quickly at times where they are often caught unaware or unprepared. You have to slow it down and allow yourself, your team, and your people the time to process the issue and triage in order to prioritize— I learned that from MASH—what needs to be done now (urgent) and what can be delayed (less urgent) until we are prepared to act appropriately.

Problems are often presented as issues—they sound better and seem more appealing to confront than problems. In actuality, they are one in the same; yet in management, we like to see ourselves as problem solvers. Have you ever heard someone referred to as an "issue solver?" No—of course not, *issues are dealt with* and *problems are solved*. We derive problem-solving from mathematics where we work to solve.

Complex problems often require stages, ample time, and real thought. Real problems and real issues need to be handled or dealt with and resolved or solved. Hence the phrase, "Problem Solved!" In two short words, we are communicating to someone or the group that—*we*—have dealt with the issue(s) at hand and rid ourselves of the obstacle(s), thus carrying out our mission to continue toward success. So how do we go about it? How do we address an issue? How do we address any issue? Does it depend on the size of the issue—whether it is small or large? Is it based on whether the issue or problem is considered material or not? These are all questions that require each of us to plan and implement action steps to reach solutions that work. The degree of structure for the decision-making model should equal the level of complexity of the problem. Simple problem—simple solution (less steps, less process); complex problem—higher degree of decision-making model and more detailed solution (more steps, more process). This means more people and resources, which tends to require committees to effectively parse out the work and study the intricacies of the problem.

Take the Iran hostage crisis that began on November 4, 1979. Here we have an example of a complex problem that required significant process and steps to solve in order to reach the only solution acceptable—ending the standoff and returning the hostages without harm.

A diplomatic standoff between the United States and Iran broke out in which fifty-two American diplomats and citizens were held hostage for 444 days that ended on January 20, 1981.[4] A group of Iranian college students belonging to the Muslim Student Followers of the Imam's Line,[5] who supported the Iranian Revolution, stormed the U.S. Embassy in Tehran. It consumed the news for the entire year of 1980. This became a major problem for the thirty-ninth president of the United States, Jimmy Carter. Political analysts cited the standoff as a major factor in the continuing downfall of Carter's presidency and his landslide loss in the 1980 presidential election— "the hostage crisis loomed large in the landslide win by Mr. Reagan, a Republican, over Democratic Incumbent Jimmy Carter in the fall of 1980. For one thing, Election Day fell on the one-year anniversary of the start of the crisis."[6]

While the Carter administration was struggling to find solutions to solve the larger problem of the fifty-two hostages, CIA operative Tony Mendez was pitching a creative idea as a solution to rescue six diplomats who were in hiding at the residence of the Canadian diplomat, Kenneth Taylor. The solutions to solve the larger problem by the administration—though broad and immediate ranging from sanctions including cutting off sales of Iranian oil and freezing Iranian assets—were ineffective and costly to the president in terms of approval ratings and reelection hopes.

> These measures did nothing to help along diplomatic negotiations for the release of the prisoners, so on April 7, 1980, 212 days after the crisis began, he announced even more drastic measures. The U.S. cut off diplomatic relations with Iran, imposed economic sanctions including cutting off food aid, closed Iranian institutions within the U.S., and embargoed all imports from Iran.[7]

The CIA on the other hand invested more time and resources in an elaborate plan that was shared with the world in 2012 with the release of the major motion picture, *Argo*,[8] starring among many well-known actors, Ben Affleck playing Tony Mendez, the CIA operative who solved the problem associated with the rescue. The problem to be solved was how to provide a cover story that was plausible in securing a safe travel route out of the country for the group. During the initial brainstorming session as depicted in the movie,[9] ideas were being bandied about from disguising the six as college students who could bike their way out—problem being—*there were no longer any foreign students permitted at that point and the Turkish border was an easy 800 km or 500 miles away.* Another idea was to identify them as part of an agricultural mission in which they would pose as inspectors to check on crops—*the problem with that idea was the time of year (winter) when crops were not present.*

In an article that appeared in the *Daily Beast*, an American news and opinion website focused on politics and pop culture, Mendez explained, "The trick was finding those kinds of jobs that give a person clout—art director, cinematographer, transportation coordinator—without the kind of marquis billing that a director or producer might get, which would be easier for the Iranians to check."[10]

> The exfiltration task was daunting—the six Americans had no intelligence background; planning required extensive coordination within the US and Canadian governments; and failure not only threatened the safety of the hostages but also posed considerable risk of worldwide embarrassment to the US and Canada. Other significant problems included overcoming Iran's strict immigration exit controls and creation of a credible cover story and supporting documentation for the six Americans.[11]

As part of their decision-making process, the group gave careful consideration of numerous options until the Argo idea emerged as the "best of the bad ideas" as stated by Mendez: "There are only bad options. It's about finding the best one." Thus began the mustering of resources and detailed planning necessary to legitimize the cover story. The production of a Hollywood movie presented the opportunity to devise an exotic cover story that was believable enough to thwart suspicions.

While the movie is entertaining and the storyline gripping, it demonstrates the difficulties and challenges associated with problem-solving for a *high-risk, high-reward* solutions. The plot unfolds with the dramatization of the true story full of fear, determination, cunning, and bravery that keeps you on the edge of your seat. The entire movie is about problem-solving; however, in this case, solving the problem meant keeping the group alive until they were out of harm's way and delivered home safely. These kinds of problems are the highest priority as human lives are at stake much like military operations. In organizations and companies, often times it is the life of the company or organization itself that hangs in the balance as critical problems emerge that require solutions that work.

So why did one solution, the "Canadian Caper" (Argo), work, while the other, sanctions, did not? While the intricacies of foreign policy are many and each case is unique with its own set of circumstances, the main difference with each solution was time. The rescue of the six was based on actions that took place "in-the-now" and a plan that once set into motion had a definitive time table—an "all or nothing proposition." Whereas the sanctions, although harmful to Iran's economy, were slower to take root and produced a *"wait-and-see* situation." Furthermore, the effects of the measures were weighed against the cost-benefit of consolidating power among Iran's new leaders over internal rivals and thus the decision to prolong the crisis by those leaders.[12]

Getting back to solutions that work—solutions are only as good as how they are acted upon and carried out. One person or team may attempt and fail while another person or team can achieve success by employing the very same solution. This underscores the value of individuals involved in the process of problem-solving. The individual or group generating the solution(s) may not be the best suited to carry out the mission. One must be trained, certified, and experienced with the task at hand in order to be successful in achieving the desired outcome(s).

Think about an NFL football team—they can run the same play and get a different result depending on the players running the play. That is the offense; however, depending on the team you are playing the defensive players can also shut down the very play that worked successfully just a week ago against a different team with less experienced and/or athletic players. That is the epitome of variables and why great coaches know how to plan ahead, execute, and adjust on the fly based on changes in coverage they see or shifts on the line with player moving prior snap. The same is true of great leaders within successful organizations. They do their homework and keep abreast of variables such as market conditions that affect their environment.

Understanding the variables that effect our environment in any industry or field requires professional development, attendance, and interaction at workshops, research, and reading to stay on top of today's issues. This is what allows us to be better problem solvers as we stay in step with the issues of the day as well as learn of similar or different problems experienced by peer groups with solutions that worked or not for them. This broadens our frame of reference and strengthens our knowledge base should we find ourselves in similar situations. This is how we retain and improve our own value to the companies and organizations we serve. When we stop learning, we stop growing—and therefore begin the process of becoming obsolete. This is a killer in management *where our success is measured daily*.

The success of any solution in the act of problem-solving is determinant by a number of factors both internal and external.

Figure 3.1   Factors that influence success or failure of problem solving solutions for organizations and businesses

Organizational Culture (Internal) plays a major role in shaping the success or failure of our solutions as it dictates the values, attitudes, and priorities that our employees live by—our creed—the beliefs or aims that guide our actions. If it is one of collaboration and teamwork, we are sure to be able to illicit the strength and support of the team in solving the problems that come our way. "In a world where change is fast and furious, the old-school approach of having leaders go off behind closed doors to solve problems is simply not enough."[13] "Instead, for today's leaders seeking to improve operations, enhance productivity, increase customer satisfaction and reap the benefits of company-wide progress, the better approach is to develop a thorough problem-solving culture that touches upon all aspects of the organization."[14]

Organizational culture starts at the top and is evidenced-based—it transcends mottos, slogans, and mission statements by staff based on evidence and reasoning. If the values of a company or organization are not upheld by its leaders, the staff are quick to realize and act accordingly. As such, it is difficult to count on staff and members of your team to go the extra mile and ensure success when they see you or other leaders living outside of the expectations set for them.

It is hard to discipline individuals for infractions of the rules that others violate on a consistent basis with no penalties or consequences. When this happens in organizations, they often find individuals who show up late, leave early, and find excuses to avoid hard work. Instead, they simply exist to collect their paychecks and whatever other benefits the company or organization offers. If left unchecked, the organization or company will eventually falter or worse go out of business.

Competition (External) remains a challenge in problem-solving as firms that compete are after the same support—whether that support is in the form of funding, market share, followers, or rankings. Organizations, both public and private, find themselves competing in the same geographic markets (international, domestic, regional, and local) in which they need to convince their shareholders or stakeholders of the *value add* they possess that makes them worth the investment.

For this reason, companies and organizations need to realize who their competitors are and how to "get a leg up" on the competition, to prosper by getting ahead, and then figuring out how to stay there. This is especially true of financing for new initiatives given limited resources for many public concerns like schools. Fundraising is equally challenging as everyone is seeking donations from the same support base of local and regional businesses. In this case, the problem to solve is figuring out how to get to those supporters in a way that convinces them to support your needs over others.

Companies looking to expand operations and grow their business often require the assistance of venture capitalists; however, again we find there are limited resources as supply and demand are again at work. Getting to the next level means competing for the capital to get them there. "In the venture market, Demand for venture capital is essentially the number of companies looking for venture funding. The Supply is the amount of venture capital investors are willing to invest in companies given a rate of return (inverse of the price at which they will invest)."[15]

Without these vital resources, we are limited in our ability to solve the problems we face today and expect to encounter in the future. Going back to chapter 1, if the "most creative person(s) in the room" belongs to your competition, you may be left with individuals who come up short in solving your organization's problems while your competitor(s) flourish. With success comes support, financing, rankings, and followers.

Funding and Resources (Internal) determine the survival of any organization. Look at research grants. Once the funding dries up, the research stops; it's that simple. While money is not always the answer or the first ingredient in the recipe for every solution, it is usually a critical component in the mix of the overall solution; if for no other reason, we need it to maintain the staff tasked with solving or implementing our solutions. Additionally, without funding we are hard-pressed to acquire, maintain, and employ those resources.

> Although your business may be based on an aesthetic vision or a personal ideal, it will only be able to operate successfully if it is financially sound. Most businesses pass through startup and growth periods spending more than they earn, however, the long-term health of any company depends on ultimately earning more money than it spends. In addition, financially viable companies must manage cash flow effectively enough to avoid debilitating finance charges and have enough capital on hand to cover basic expenses.[16]

While funding is critical to any organization, other characteristics are just as important to problem-solving, including creativity, ingenuity, resourcefulness, determination, and grit. These attributes often lead the way to successful solutions that work; however, while passion can overcome lack of resources in the short term, in order to achieve sustainability, organizations need to ensure they have enough liquidity, assets, and reserves in order to go the distance.

Supply and Demand (External) remains a constant factor in our ability to procure the resources we need at a price we can afford. While every company works to build relationships with quality vendors, suppliers, and professionals for materials, supplies, and services, the cost and availability of those items is determined by factors such as quantity, quality, availability, timing, and delivery. Any basic course in economics will refer to the *equilibrium price* or market price where the *quantity* of goods supplied is equal to the *quantity* of goods demanded. This is the point at which the demand and supply curves in the market intersect. Why does this matter in problem-solving? Because "you need what you need"—"when you need it," and if you cannot afford to purchase due to cash flow issues, tight budgets, or time constraints, your problems just get bigger.

That is why it is important to expand the group of suppliers through consortiums and memberships in regional and national cooperatives that broaden purchase options and secure better pricing for goods and services that have already been bid. This is especially critical for public bodies that are held to purchasing standards set up by state and federal governments.

Private businesses as well are better served to have established purchasing discounts and terms from preferred distributors. Again as put forward in the planning stage, these relationships become vital when time is of the essence and demand limits supply.

Policy and Procedures (Internal) provide the guidance and direction for day-to-day operations and ensure compliance with laws and regulations. Effective policy is invaluable in problem-solving as it provides clear direction for solutions needed to address concerns that arise each day. Without clear policy or lacking procedures, just the opposite is true; we find ourselves lacking the backup or support of our decisions when challenged.

Policy shapes our decisions and guides us on addressing the challenges of a changing environment as long as those policies are kept up to date and reflective of the changes in our environments. "The enterprise has little influence on the environment and therefore, it is important for the company to identify with the environment of its operation and devise its policies in relation to the forces in that environment."[17]

Government Regulation (External) controls many aspects of how businesses and organizations operate in the form of rules and regulations, code requirements, interest rates, tax codes, labor standards, and environmental standards, just to name a few. Awareness, understanding, and adherence to those rules and regulations are necessary to succeed—the alternative is problems that if left unsolved will lead to failure. "Whether you like regulations or not, compliance is important. Staying on top of the rules (which are often changing) is essential to maintaining a competitive edge. Failing to do so means incurring penalties and potential legal issues, which could cause you to fall behind your competition."[18]

Quality of Staff (Internal)—solutions to problems are only as good as the staff we have to execute them. When it comes to solving problems we want the "A" team, not the "B" team, and certainly not the "C" team. The strength of the team comes from coaching, training, communicating, and understanding. Our best leaders are mentors who provide these qualities in ways that are appreciated and respected for their sage advice and honest feedback.

When we appreciate and respect those who lead us, we develop closer relationships and therefore extend ourselves and our effort beyond merely showing up and doing what needs doing. Think about any relationship you have experienced in your life. When you like someone, you are quick to do for them. When they appreciate you, you feel good. It is a simple response to our human nature. That is the first step in cultivating a team that enjoys being there; however, we are talking about work, not camp. This is where respect and discipline enter the scene.

Great teams communicate well, focus on goals and objectives, share the load, hold one another accountable, exchange knowledge, support each other, accept feedback, and look to improve. Great leaders find ways to bring them together through fun and interesting team-building opportunities and adventures. Take a day away from the office with your team and explore who they are and what makes them unique, what are their commonalities, strengths, weaknesses, and how we can harness the power of the team by drawing on the combined strengths, while shoring up any weaknesses.

As we struggle with *what's next*, we need to keep our teams solid, active, and connected. Look for available resources to assist in this aim. They can be found with a quick search and applied to your teams by customizing the exercises to your groups and their particular needs. Keep in mind the organization's culture, mission, and vision when planning exercises that allow them to (1) believe in the cause, (2) understand their importance, and (3) value the strength of the team.

MindTools.com is an online source for leaders that shares creative ideas, tools, and valuable insights with a wide range of high-quality, practical, on-demand resources. Below are key takeaways for ensuring quality team-building experiences:

> Team building can only occur when relevant and timely activities that address specific needs that are part of your organization's culture. One-off exercises can help with this, but they are not a shortcut to success.[19]
>
> The purpose of team building activities is to motivate your people to work together, to develop their strengths, and to address any weaknesses. So, any team building exercise should encourage collaboration rather than competition.[20]
>
> Be sure to incorporate team building into your workplace routines and practices. For example, get to know your people better, work toward common goals, develop their skills, and make the extra effort to connect with your virtual team members.[21]

Available Workforce (External)—nothing impacts our ability to succeed like the availability of quality people to staff our organizations when needed.

Even as we employ strategies and launch initiatives to retain employees by maintaining competitive salary and benefits packages, providing growth opportunities and a host of other comps, people leave for reasons that we cannot control: retirement, relocation, health, family leave, or other personal reasons. Their departure requires us to find suitable replacements and the availability of quality labor has a direct impact on ability to staff.

During periods of strong economic activity, unemployment rates fall as the economy expands; this results in a shrinking pool of available labor. Recognizing labor trends in the work force allows organizations to prepare for changes in staffing needs by aligning planned expansions with periods of labor abundance or developing partnerships to tap into new labor pools during shortages.

Equally important when analyzing trends in any market is to account for spikes when they happen as they are often quick, abrupt, and unforeseen. Understanding the cause-and-effect relationship allows us to make quick decisions that are knowledgeable, fact-based, and supported with data to plan appropriate solutions until market conditions return to normal.

Start-ups for instance or those looking to open their own business would need to realize that although the unemployment numbers are currently very high, likened to the "Great Depression," they are expected to be temporary and those sidelined will be returning to jobs they still hold claim to.

Case in point: The unemployment rate from January 2018 to January 2019[22] hovered around 4 percent, and held steady just under 4 percent for the next thirteen months before jumping to 14.7 percent in April 2020[23] due to impact of COVID-19 shutdowns, which closed operations and furloughed workers.

Until we see the final effects of the relaxation of the shutdown orders and social distancing guidelines, we cannot properly analyze the true unemployment figures or their impact on the available labor.

Chapter 4

The Power of Reason

Reason is defined as "the power of comprehending, inferring, or thinking especially in orderly rational ways."[1] It is based on *logic* or as the early Greeks referred to it—*logos*. In their explanation they considered it; *logos* as reason by its very definition. To take it a step further, reason derives its power from the thought process in coming to a clear decision that is well supported in logic—the "proper exercise of the mind."[2] This mental workout can be quick or exhaustive depending on the size of the problem; however, the task requires the same degree of deep thought and consideration of variables in coming up with solutions that don't just work but improve the situation. Decisions that do not require any real thought are not problems but simply tasks that need to be completed. "Anyone can hold the helm when the sea is calm."[3]

When we insert reason into our decision making, we guard against failure and improve our outcomes by ensuring our actions are well thought through and well thought out. When we check our thoughts with others—bouncing ideas—we gather instant feedback that serves to only strengthen our ultimate plans. While this seems straightforward and most leaders believe they do this often and well, it just is not so. If it were, we would only see success.

Not to be confused with setbacks or failed attempts to solve; trial and error is an important component and necessary to solve some of our biggest problems—that's determination, that's tenacity—"If we can't find a way we will make one"—Hannibal.

Collaboration is not merely getting people into a room and telling them about your idea and then proceeding to direct them on how to achieve it—that is simply gathering. When we allow the free flow of ideas that challenge, analyze, pull apart, and modify those ideas to improve their impact, we have a collaborative environment. When free thinking is encouraged and rewarded, we have empowerment. When ideas begin to morph into realistic plans through creativity, we possess six key elements for success in problem-solving—*creativity, ability, reality, objectivity, viability,* and *actionability.*

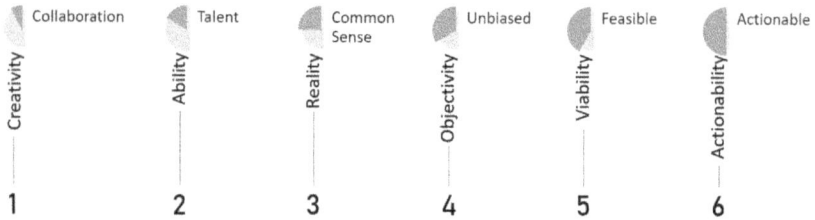

Creativity	Ability	Reality	Objectivity	Viability	Actionability
Collaboration	Talent	Common Sense	Unbiased	Feasible	Actionable
1	2	3	4	5	6

1. **Creativity** needs ***collaboration*** to generate *big ideas* that go beyond the initial thoughts of any one person.
2. **Ability,** in the form of bright ***talent***, provides the energy to generate solutions.
3. **Reality** is what keeps our ideas actionable as they are grounded in ***common sense***.
4. **Objectivity** provides an ***unbiased*** result needed to remain free from bias to solve our problems.
5. **Viability** is achieved by ensuring our ideas are *feasible*, that they can live on after analysis, questioning, and study.
6. **Actionability** is the quality or state of being ***actionable***, made ready and available for implementation.

Reason serves to provide the objectivity needed in determining the availability of resources to achieve viability for any company or business. Planning becomes the necessity to make our ideas actionable.

So why is problem-solving such a challenge? Because after we properly identify the problem and decide on the process to utilize in preparation of our approach, we need to consider all the *variables* and ensure we haven't missed any. Is this possible—yes or we would never solve any problem; but it can be challenging and more often than not requires many attempts to get to the ultimate goal. This involves logical thinking.

"Logical thinking is the act of analyzing a situation and coming up with a sensible solution. Similar to critical thinking, logical thinking requires the use of reasoning skills to study a problem objectively, which will allow you to make a rational conclusion about how to proceed. When you use the facts available to you to address a problem you may be facing at work, for example, you are using logical reasoning skills."[4]

Let's look at a few specific examples.

CASE STUDY | SUMMIT HIGH SCHOOL CULINARY ARTS REDESIGN 2018 (ORIGINAL FOODS PROGRAM)

- ***The problem:*** Code Violations from Improper Exhaust in Foods Program Room
- ***The solution:*** $1.3M State of the Art Culinary Lab

In the 2016–2017 school year, the program was cited by the Summit Fire Code Official for improper ventilation, discharge, and fire suppression. The citation noted: Range hoods need to discharge outside the building—NOT IN THE ROOM.

- *Exhaust hood systems need to be capable of exhausting in excess of 400 cubic feet per minute.*
- *Ducts serving range hoods shall not terminate in an attic or crawl space or areas inside the building.*

> Only 1 of 4 workstations had an appropriate hood and it was not ducted properly. The remaining ranges all vented into the room. It had been that way for years; however, it was not picked up in prior inspections as the room had served originally as a Home Economics class with basic cooking and it was always clean and well maintained so it appeared to be fine on the surface. At a quick glance it looked like a typical room for basic cooking classes and never attracted any close attention on walkthroughs. That all changed one day when the hood that did exhaust was clogging and appeared to be working improperly. As the fire code official began to dig deeper the violations began to mount and the program was shut down.

My facilities director notified me of the problem and we met on site with the building principal, the director of fine performing arts, and the two teachers for the program. The initial estimate for repairs to bring hood units up to code was about $100,000 or $25,000 per range. The original Home Economics design build (circa 2001) was dated and not in line with the progression of the foods program that currently occupied the space fifteen years later. That was just the equipment costs—add labor and trades involved and the estimate could go to $150,000. We had to immediately suspend cooking and adjust the lesson plans to finish out the school year (*its own problem solve*) while we worked on solving the problem to clear the violations and restore the program for the following school year. Fortunately, we were already in May and the teachers were great in providing a quick work-around and adjustments to continue the course until June.

Over the next few weeks, we got estimates for the repairs, consulted with our architects, and began brainstorming solutions to the venting issue that appeared to become more complicated as the room was on the first floor and could only be vented up through another room and then out through the roof. Perhaps that is why it wasn't properly vented to begin with.

The immediate question that faced us was whether we should sink $150,000 into the repairs of the existing layout or consider a remodel and revamp the entire program. The existing space was dated with aged countertops, sinks, and cabinetry not to mention a poor design in which all workstations faced the walls. In contrast, we had an opportunity to modernize the space with a new Foods program inclusive of *chef stations* designed to promote a culinary career track. With a new open floor plan, we could allow students to prep, cook, and learn all the while seeing the instructors for instruction and demonstrations. We put our estimate of between $300,000 and $400,000 figuring we could do much of the construction in-house through our maintenance team to include demolition, plumbing, and electric.

The timing was great as the popular TV shows such as Top Chef had been running for about a decade and gaining in popularity. At the same time, the Partnership for Assessment of Readiness for College and Careers (PARCC) had dominated curriculum development with a focus on college and career readiness.

Instead of seeing this as a *problem*, we began to see it as an *opportunity* to improve and modernize the learning space while upgrading the student experience and providing a real career option. The vision was simple— take a tired outdated program and reengineer the curriculum to match the upscaled culinary track we proposed. With support from the superintendent, we approached the board of education with a plan to invest approximately $400,000 into the project. It was met with expected enthusiasm and we were off to the races. Our first action was to meet with the architects and form a design committee in order to come up with some basic plans.

Over the next six months, we conducted site visits at two major county vocational programs, held various meetings with the architectural team, fine arts supervisor, and select staff members at the high school. All the while gathering information and reviewing other culinary-type programs and designs from school districts across the county.

We suffered our first major setback around May of 2017 when the engineering department at EI Associates began drafting the mechanical drawings for the necessary fire suppression upgrades to meet the required code—they came in around $160,000 that would later track with the actual bid. On the heels of the mechanical work came a price tag of $140,000 for cooling/heating ($90k) and exhaust work ($60k) as the system was required to be separated from rest of building due to potential smoke/fire and required make-up air for ventilation. Together, these costs represented 75 percent of our budget and we hadn't even added in the plumbing, electric, and demolition estimate—another $90,000 thus consuming 98 percent of our overall budget and we hadn't even begun to select materials or appliances. These were the *variables* that none of us saw at the time as they were hidden. We were simply looking at what was in front of us and thinking along the lines of a kitchen remodel with major upgrades. Even our architects were surprised at the level of code requirements as the appliances necessary to support the high-end program were tied to commercial-grade applications.

Our second setback occurred a few months later when we realized that we did not have the appropriate square footage in the existing room to house the other half of the instructional program, a fashion arts class, that included more than twenty sewing machines and storage requirements that outstripped our capacity needs for the culinary equipment and basic cooking supplies. That *solution* would come months later from a conversation with the prior principal who had recently retired that led to consolidation of two photography labs confirmed by the current principal as that program had moved to a digital platform.

Our dream was dying, and we still hadn't solved the original problem as we simply got a deferment from the fire inspector after a lot of arm twisting, political wrangling, and a promise of a corrective action plan that included sealed architectural plans. Bottom line, we were running out of time and our options were vanishing. We began to consider scraping the program.

This is not untypical when it comes to problem-solving as many solutions present additional problems that ultimately lead to doing nothing commonly accepted as "the status quo." Ask any superintendent or architect who successfully achieved a multimillion-dollar expansion through an approved referendum. Ask the business administrator who worked on the financing plans and facility approvals to make it a reality and you will find more often than not that they achieved this success after many meetings, setbacks, communication campaigns, and countless redesigns, scale backs, additions, and trade-offs. But at the heart of every successful endeavor is *problem-solving*. These leaders and the professionals they work with had the ability to join *creativity* with *necessity* and package it in a way that made sense to achieve the support—that is how plans become reality.

Creativity is what gets us over the hurdles we face whether we find ways to jump higher, lower the hurdle, or simply develop a plan to go around. Twenty years ago, I was working with the same architectural team in Montague, the highest elevation within New Jersey at an altitude of 1,803 feet (550 meter) above sea level. It is also the northernmost municipality in the state and known for its rocky terrain that can be found throughout High Point National Park located in the heart of the township. We were designing a new parking lot and knowing this we incorporated contingency into our overall budget for any rock encountered during our excavation but got stopped in our tracks as the contractor on the job presented us with a rock outcropping that not only was massive but also had an adjacent utility pole that would need to be relocated. That part we knew as the drawings had included the new positioning of the pole—what we didn't know, what we thought we prepared for (variables) was the extent of the rock outcropping, which seemed to resemble an iceberg with the largest part underneath the surface. So what did we do—after an afternoon of potential field expedient alterations to the plan, we decided to incorporate it into the design and introduced an island that not only negated the need to break the rock but also added a natural element to the design. This also meant we no longer needed to relocate the utility pole, saving both time and money. Once in a while, I'll take a drive up that way and pull through the parking lot to admire the result and always think back on our ability to solve.

REVIVAL OF THE DREAM—A Confluence of Fortuitous Events

Around the same time in September of 2016, I accompanied my wife to a cooking demonstration fundraiser sponsored by Hackensack University Medical Center. As fate would have it, Kevin Felice, corporate chef for 40 North Restaurant Group, was the master chef for the evening. The group had just opened a new restaurant in Summit, The Office Tavern and Grill, and Kevin was heavily involved in making that start successful. I was aware of the restaurant but not the company. Talk about fortuitous timing! I instantly saw the potential of Kevin and 40 North as a community resource.

As I watched the demonstration, my interests went beyond the food and dishes that were being prepared to the design layout of the kitchen and the flat panel displays that projected different camera angles from the countertop prep to the cooking range and on the chef himself as he detailed each of the steps in the process. I immediately rose and started taking pictures with my iPhone including video to capture every angle of the layout, design elements, and appliances including the workstations and seating for the participants (students). My wife was surprised at the level of interest I displayed as cooking is not my thing. What she did not know until later that evening was my true motivation. I was soaking in the setting and setup with an eye toward a renewed vision of what this could mean for our culinary project and how this setup mirrored the high-end look that we needed to transform our program not into a "scratch kitchen" but more in line with a culinary theater hosting audiences of up to twenty-six students at long worktables that could be easily grouped into longer communal tables for various events. Visiting chefs could perform multicourse cooking demos that we could display in the room on large screens and simultaneously broadcast over our district channel from our state-of-the art media literacy studio—another successful project we brought on line in 2009. The excitement was high and the idea was revived. It became more of a reality when Kevin agreed to join our team and lend his expertise to revamping our plan.

While *reason* derives its power from the *thought process*, *optimism* fuels the *passion* that turns our most favorable dreams into actions—our plans. *Practicality* readies those plans making them real—as opposed to *speculation* or *abstract thought*.

What helped was the strength of the team—we had to think bigger. In the words of my secretary and die-hard Mets fan, "Think big or go home!" We had been working off the premise of interjecting a *culinary track* into the *basic foods program* we had to move beyond the track consideration and turn it into a full-blown culinary arts program. With that realization, we began to think bigger and expand our knowledge of culinary programs, which to that point had included site visits to the two vocational programs and a couple of neighboring high schools that provided more vocational settings with stainless steel-dominant kitchens providing an industrial layout you would find in a process kitchen. We were not looking to compete with these type of programs and really wanted a blended approach that would provide a high-end demonstration kitchen much like you experience while taking a cooking class. This is where our superintendent came in handy with his progressive thinking and enthusiastic support that led to a visit to the Culinary Institute of America, which was literally in our backyard a short drive over the border in neighboring Hyde Park, New York.

Our design committee had transitioned into an exploration committee and a month later we were back in action at the CIA meeting with the program director and observing top-rated instruction in design kitchens, prep areas, and state-of-the art learning spaces ending our tour in their world-renowned restaurants that provide an array of culinary experiences, from modern French to farm-to-table and from authentic Italian to new global flavors.

Our final challenge was funding, after we solved the first two setbacks and reengaged the board and community with the Culinary Arts program through a new public presentation in May of 2018. The plan was sound, but it came with a hefty price tag and a challenge to find the funding. Any additional resources directed to this program would come at the cost of other programs that were equally important and while the board supported the plan they were not ready to commit the additional funds from our regular operating budget. Our Capital Reserve funds were adequate to meet the first $400,000 since it was attributed to required work to address the code violations but beyond that we needed to find alternative funding.

We found ourselves about $600,000 short to cover the funds necessary to meet the remaining constructions costs that included the commercial-grade convections ovens, refrigeration units, and appliances like dishwashers. Our technology team had been added to the design committee to work out the technical specs for the cameras and flat panel units that would retract into the ceiling. The ceiling heights presented its own challenge due to height requirements for ductwork and sight lines for instruction. The architectural team solved that challenge but it all added to the construction budget.

As managers, we all operate under the concept of thinking outside the box when problem-solving and this problem—lack of funding—was not unique; however, the fix was totally unique and way outside the box. We came up with a great idea. This is where being close to the front line on budget and understanding the details of the various accounts and funds we manage was invaluable. Since the space was designed for specialized instruction related to food preparation and culinary cooking on a scale necessary for restaurants, we approached the Food Service Management Company that ran our district food service to test the plausibility of using the space after school hours as a dual training site to allow their staff to meet the training requirements set forth by the Department of Agriculture and the National Food Service program. This was key in accessing profits we had earned over the previous years that could only be reinvested in food service activities as the funds resided in a separate enterprise fund. That would get us another $400,000 but we needed state and auditor approval, which we accomplished in a matter of weeks as the plan was sound.

The next $200,000 we came by applying the same principal thanks to our auditors who pointed out our summer enrichment program (FLASH) utilized the space for foods programs as well and the profit in that fund was just over the amount needed. They too would be able to benefit from the new space and as such became another part of the puzzle to get us to the $600,000 needed.

Construction started on June 4, 2018, and we opened the program in September of 2018. The project spanned three fiscal years (FY16–FY18) from initial discussion to final completion including three redesigns and three budgetary revisions along with countless meetings and more than a few site visits. Today, it is one of our proudest additions to our high school program recently ranked #19 in New Jersey and #448 nationwide by U.S. News & World Report Best High Schools.[5]

I have been guided in my decision making for the past thirty years with a simple phrase I offer to my team and colleagues that puts things in perspective and answers the question of what we should do—that phrase, "Common Sense" rules the day! When things make sense, they are easy to see and even easier to understand—that not only makes sense it means it is based on logic and it is easy to sell or in our case explain to others who we are looking to get "buy-in" from. As leaders, this is critical to achieve the ultimate success or based on the premise of this book—solve the problems that confront us. If it doesn't make sense, then why we would do it?

Part 2

PROBLEM SOLVING

Chapter 5

The Importance of Research

"If it ain't broke – don't fix it."

As leaders, we have heard this aphorism all too often from those who are resistant to change and who cling to this principle as a favorite maxim akin to "Don't count your chickens before they hatch." Aphorisms are a great way to impart a quick message since they are concise and memorable, much like proverbs, which impart wisdom or practical truth. While each of these statements applies at times and should be heeded, they are not always applicable to every situation we attempt to improve—especially in the face of problem-solving when things aren't okay or we do need to fix what is broken. Counting chickens can merely be a sign of optimism related to rewards from taking *acceptable risks*: ***"from nothing comes nothing"*** or ***"nothing ventured nothing gained."***

When the time comes to find a fix—when we have determined that the system is broken—we begin to *problem-solve*, and in doing so, we need to understand what we are dealing with to get at the heart of the problem. This requires a depth of learning that goes beyond the surface of the problem, including the variables we touched on in the last chapter. This requires knowledge as "Knowledge is Power."

I love quick phrases that we see all around us in use today that are tied to this concept of "knowledge being powerful"—Channel 12 News' in New Jersey, New York, and Connecticut's tag line for local traffic and weather, "Know before you go!"—iSpot.tv, the industry standard in real-time media measurement, tracked 404 nationally aired TV ad campaigns for NBC's "The More You Know" reporting 396 airings in the past 30 days earning an airing rank of #1,350 with a spend ranking of #3,219 as compared to all other advertisers[1], representing a significant investment for NBC.

It is all about learning to gather a deeper understanding that increases our knowledge, thus allowing us to apply that knowledge in solving our problems or in the case of local traffic and weather, avoiding the problems in the first place. Science is a critical field in gathering that understanding and promoting practical application to solve many of our problems whether they are Formal Sciences (mathematics and logic), Natural Sciences (biology, chemistry, physics or earth), Engineering and Technology, Medical and Health Sciences, Agricultural Sciences, and Social Sciences or Humanities. This realization is the key driver behind the focus on STEAM Education, an approach to learning that uses Science, Technology, Engineering, the Arts, and Mathematics as access points for guiding student inquiry, dialogue, and critical thinking.[2]

"Francis Bacon was the first to formalize the concept of a true scientific method, but he didn't do so in a vacuum. The work of Nicolaus Copernicus (1473–1543) and Galileo Galilei (1564–1642) influenced Bacon tremendously."[3]

"Scientia potentia est," a Latin aphorism meaning "knowledge is power," is commonly attributed to Sir Francis Bacon, lawyer, philosopher, former Attorney General (1613), and Lord Chancellor of England (1618).[4] Although his political and public career ended in disgrace in 1621,[5] he remains a heavily cited figure throughout modern history in recognition of the meaning behind the quote and the power derived from research attributed to the *scientific method.*

> The scientific method is an empirical method of acquiring knowledge that has characterized the development of science since at least the 17th century. It involves careful observation, applying rigorous skepticism about what is observed, given that cognitive assumptions can distort how one interprets the observation. It involves formulating hypotheses, via induction, based on such observations; experimental and measurement-based testing of deductions drawn from the hypotheses; and refinement (or elimination) of the hypotheses based on the experimental findings. These are principles of the scientific method, as distinguished from a definitive series of steps applicable to all scientific enterprises.[1][2][3][6]

Research is how we *dig in* or *dive deep* into the data we are presented with—the *how, when, and why* things work that allows us to truly understand what we are dealing with not just the symptoms. We all focus on the *how* and *why*; however, the *when* is equally important when considering cyclical versus random events. The *when* allows us to tie the cause to a specific incident or change in market conditions such as major events like implementation of new standards in testing, regulatory changes with the passage of a new law or bigger impacts such as 911 in New York City or other acts of terrorism, regional conflicts, catastrophic weather events, or larger global events like the recent COVID-19 pandemic affecting supply chain availability around the globe.

Back to the *cause and effect*, we often know the effect(s) of our problems as they are clearly visible in the form of incidents, reports, notifications, and observations. What we need to discover is the *how* and the *why* as well as *when* (*the cause*) to ensure we are not creating or generating more damaging effects. This underscores the importance of research and reliance on knowledge.

Problem-solving skills are in high demand in any industry as we seek to find solutions to problems that continuously confront managers and teams to maintain and improve our processes and meet the challenges that emerge daily. Research can be as easy as doing a google search; however, more difficult issues require data analysis tied to research methods that incorporate qualitative and quantitative approaches.

A good example of a qualitative research method in problem-solving is an exit interview, where we are attempting to find out why (*the cause*) an employee or group of employees are leaving in order to address excessive turnover (*the effect*). Larger issues a company or organization may be facing such as falling ratings, loss of market share, or declining profits might turn to focus groups to gain a broader understanding of the issues driving the adverse action. Both of these methods allow researchers to explore a topic in depth. You can also collect qualitative data from customer interactions, employee feedback, or surveys. Online survey tools are readily available today and often free to use.

Five of the top free online survey tools in no particular order[7]:

1. Google Forms. Does your organization live and die by your Google Drive? If you already have a Google account, this could be an easy winner and user friendly as those within your organization have already adapted to Google for everything from Calendar to Docs to Sheets and even Slides.
2. Survey Monkey. Despite the limitations of its free plans, SurveyMonkey continues to be popular, thanks to its intuitive interface and brand recognition. Notable clients include HP, GoPro, Progressive, and Lyft.[8]
3. Typeform. Allows you to engage your audience with conversational forms and surveys that get more data. Partnerships with Unsplash and Pexels provide free access to millions of images and video content that can be embedded in your surveys.
4. Zoho Survey. Part of the Zoho suite of apps that caters to sales, HR, IT, finance, and virtually any kind of business—allows users to create surveys in minutes that reach their audiences on every device and view results graphically and in real time. Customers include big names like Netflix, Amazon, Facebook, and Change.org.

5. SurveyGizmo. Takes data out of dashboards and puts it into the hands of people who take action. As with (Google Forms), they offer unlimited questions and Excel exports in their free plan. Clients include Disney, Salesforce, Verizon, and The Home Depot.

Quantitative approach methods involve quantitative reasoning as utilized by the National GRE® General Test that expects test takers to model and solve problems using quantitative, or mathematical, methods[9].

Surveys, however, can also provide data that is measurable and more important comparable in determining areas of deficiency as well as strengths when compared to industry benchmarks and comparison groups.

Comparative data within any industry allows companies and organizations to look beyond the numbers (data) derived from internal or external reports on the organization's performance such as income or P&L statement or audits. Numbers in isolation are meaningless. We can see an increase in sales or a decrease in costs but unless we have a benchmark for comparisons we do not know if we are performing ahead or behind the competition. Moreover, data allows us to look back at our own performance to compare similar periods from prior years (*the when*).

Let's say an organization realized it is spending more each year on legal costs. It is determined to be problematic as the comptroller reports that the expenditures related to this line item of the budget is constantly requiring transfers to cover the costs in excess of its budget. If it is determined to be a "*one-off*" resulting from a recognizable hit such as a large settlement or protracted lawsuit, it would be covered in a briefing to senior executives and reported to the Board of Directors. Depending on the extent of the impact, it would undoubtedly be mentioned in the financials of the Annual Report or Audit dependent on the reporting requirements of the Financial or Governmental Accounting Standards Board (FASB or GASB).

If the increase is not linked to a single event (*one-off*), then the organization would need to complete a quick analysis to determine the magnitude and extent of the rise in legal expenses in order to graph enough data to determine the trend. Once this is accomplished, they would need to examine the determinants of the increase. For instance, is the increase in legal costs due to an increase in the volume of lawsuits? Is the increase based on the amount in dollars of damages sought or simply an increase in attorney billing based on more interactions (phone calls, research, filings) or time in the courtroom (litigation)?

These are all effects that are easy to distinguish. The next task in solving the problem is to determine the cause—why are they seeing an increase? The data in this case is quantifiable as we can determine the frequency (number of suits) and severity (amount of damages sought) and, more importantly, the amount of settlements or judgments. Once the data is analyzed and graphs and charts are prepared to display that data, we are able to quantify the damage but still haven't addressed the problem. Why is the organization being impacted with higher-than-normal legal fees?

That is where comparative data comes in as the organization has the ability to benchmark itself against its peers to find out if it is experiencing a problem unique to its organization or if it is experiencing a problem that is hitting the industry as a whole. This is especially critical based on the industry you are in and the expected rate of lawsuits for that industry.

In 2005, industries with the highest average number of proceedings were health care, manufacturing, and energy.[10] On average, U.S. companies filed two-and-a-half times the number of lawsuits that UK companies did. U.S. companies also initiated eight times as many arbitrations as UK companies. According to the 2005 survey conducted by Fulbright & Jaworski L.L.P, a global law firm headquartered in Houston, Texas, with offices in more than 11 major U.S. cities and more than 30 countries around the globe—electronic discovery was the number one new litigation related issue for companies with revenues over $100 million.[11]

Therefore, in our example, if the organization belonged to one of these industries experiencing larger-than-normal lawsuits related to electronic discovery, then they were not alone and simply experiencing what at the time was becoming a new trend.

While the increase in lawsuits may be connected to the industry they belong to, they should be looking at the success rate in defending claims compared to their peers and whether they need to look at changing their legal strategy and perhaps the legal team or law firm if they are performing poorly compared to their peers in defending like claims.

With respect to the research identifying *electronic discovery* as the number one challenge facing organizations in 2005, part of the solution to reduce legal costs would need to include a focus on professional development and strategies designed to minimize exposure moving forward by taking greater care in what was recorded in email, and other electronic records.

This challenge remains today and affects all organizations, private and public, with equally damaging potential requiring a deeper dive into this cause. Electronic discovery has ballooned given the rate, speed, and ease of technology, with more information than ever being recorded and stored electronically. The ease in which we can jot down our thoughts, notes, and comments in electronic form puts us, and the organizations we work for, at a substantial risk that can be extremely damaging if we fail to safeguard those thoughts, notes, and comments by ensuring they are professional, appropriate, and recorded with the knowledge that they are a public or business record and discoverable.

CDS (Complete Discovery Source) is a global leader in legal data management, providing services to law firms, government agencies, and corporations in the form of defensible support for litigation and investigations. They define eDiscovery and what it encompasses as follows:

> Electronic discovery (sometimes known as e-discovery, ediscovery, eDiscovery, or e-Discovery) is the electronic aspect of identifying, collecting and producing electronically stored information (ESI) in response to a request for production in a law suit or investigation. ESI includes, but is not limited to, emails, documents, presentations, databases, voicemail, audio and video files, social media, and web sites.[12]

How do organizations avoid or reduce this risk? It starts with *acceptable use of* policies and keeping personal devices separate from business devices—once you comingle them they become fair game.

The research conducted in the above case regarding legal costs is a good example of the importance of problem-solving, or in this case identifying not only what the problem stems from but how to solve it both now and going forward to improve the organization's outlook in this area.

SOAS University of London is the leading Higher Education institution in Europe specializing in the study of Asia, Africa, and the Near and Middle East. They qualify research by dividing it into two types: "pure or basic" and "applied research" in order to make a distinction between research that is carried out to further our knowledge and that which seeks to apply pre-existing knowledge to real-world problems[13]. This thought process accentuates the purpose of research—"problem-solving".

While every problem in business is not devastating, it can be debilitating, leading to costly fixes or extended periods of downtime or work stoppages.

Technology is another clear example of the need for continuous problem-solving based on knowledge gained through ongoing research. Computer networks are constantly evolving to keep pace with changing demands, if not they fail under the strain of those demands that lead to breakdowns and delays organizations cannot afford. Mobility demands, adaptability, scalability, and online requirements continue to present challenges disrupting today's enterprises.

Today when the Internet goes down, office work comes to a halt as individuals begin restarting computers and pounding keys to check the access before grabbing the phone to call IT. In many instances, that is met with increased frustration as many phone lines today are joined with the Internet through VoIP phone service so they go out as well. By staying ahead of these types of stoppages or down periods we are constantly problem-solving as we look to identify potential problems and provide solutions in advance of the problem(s).

If we have done our jobs correctly, we stave off problems and ensure maximum efficiency in the form of preventative maintenance, or forward thinking. Improvements to our networks mean ensuring these types of problems do not happen and even if they do, they are short lived or minimal in nature. Exceptional IT personnel are adept at this and the really good ones find creative ways to guard against disruptions by planning for the what if's and yet when the systems do go down they are masters at problem-solving to find creative and quick ways to restore those networks and get everyone back in business as fast as possible. This is where the knowledge gained from research pays off the same way as a surgeon who keeps up with medical procedures through reading journals that give them the ability to stay on top of their game and perform complicated surgeries based on a deeper understanding of challenge(s) confronting them.

Deep understanding of any problem requires knowledge of the challenge facing us. This is true of any field or discipline in any organization.

Knowledge is power, and research is the means to acquire it. Research begins when we want to know or need to know something. Study is the process to enhance our learning whether we are a student, journeyman, pioneer, or researcher. The result is the knowledge gained in the process that increases our understanding and provides us with the data and information needed for problem-solving and making intelligent fact-based decisions.

Chapter 6

The Importance of Networking

Think of networking like a giant family. Families help each other and look out for one another. Growing up in the Garden State (NJ) in the 1960s and being Italian meant large families. My father was one of six and I had more cousins than I can remember with two of my uncles and one of my aunts having multiple kids from second marriages. Every Sunday we would drive to my grandparents' house in Totowa and spend the day and most of the evening with my cousins, aunts, uncles, and my two brothers. By the end of the eight-hour visit, we would eat, pray, play, and network. Many jobs were filled in that living room and around the dining room table problems were solved, guidance was given, and names and numbers were exchanged.

While we were outside playing between meals, my parents, aunts, and uncles were talking about everything from "us" to the economy, from politics to pensions, and solving the problems of their time. Many job opportunities came out of those Sunday get-togethers as networking served to provide the necessary leads to point us in the right direction to find a good match—my father landed jobs at Thomas', Nabisco, and many machine shops; twelve years later, my older brother would get his start as an apprentice in the Painters union courtesy of my uncle, aunt Dolly's husband who was a business manager in the Local and knew they were looking for good workers. Four years later, he would help my younger brother find work through the Pipefitters union based on his mechanical skills, strength, and troubleshooting abilities. That's how it worked back then as families tried to match individual skills and interests with opportunities that led to jobs along with hard work, determination, and checking the want ads—everybody knew somebody and those with the best connections (networking) became extremely important.

While times have changed and families have become smaller, the need for a network is greater than ever. Networking is about building and maintaining relationships—knowing who's who and what they do—and more importantly how they can be beneficial. Networking is all about mutual aid—having the ability to respond to others in need and being able to call upon them when you need help. Building them is an art in itself—it's about listening and communicating to go beyond being an acquaintance and turning them into contacts. That is how we level up as an influencer and gain access to more resources.

It is known as the network effect.

> As our network expands, so does our influence based on the connections we now have access to. The chances for connection among experts, opinion leaders, colleagues, mentors, and other valuable resources, increase with every new connection we make based on their experiences, location, area of study, and knowledge bank. Each node stimulates an exponential growth of influence as we add more and more activations. It maps out the nodes (individuals or groups) and the links (relationships or interactions) that connect them.

We accomplish this by making it more personal, getting to know them, and allowing them to get to know us. Once you have pierced the surface of simply knowing who someone is, you make a personal connection that adds a degree of personalized contact that over time develops a deeper bond. That doesn't mean we are going to become personal friends with everyone we do business with; it means that we will have better contacts based on our ability to socialize and share our skills, knowledge, and expanded connections as we navigate the challenging and changing environments we must learn to master.

Networking opportunities are all around us and we can never have too many connections. Whenever individuals go through something together, it ties them to an event that they will always and forever have in common such as school, college or graduate school, military service, volunteerism, campaigns, community service, church, or work. Each of these life events creates opportunities to make friends and acquaintances that offer crossover opportunities to add to our network based on their personal and professional experiences. With that in mind, we should consider who makes sense to add to our network and having those shared experiences makes it all the easier to find the common ground in reaching out if it's been a while.

Generally, the longer the experience the deeper the bond; however, based on the degree of emotion tied to the event even short-lived, we bond—the more emotional, the more memorable. "A normal function of emotion is to enhance memory in order to improve recall of experiences that have importance or relevance for our survival. Emotion acts like a highlighter that emphasizes certain aspects of experiences to make them more memorable. Memory formation involves registering information, processing and storage, and retrieval."[1]

Building stronger networks comes down to two basic fundamentals: first, considerations for making beneficial connections; and second, finding ways to achieve it. A thoughtful approach to building stronger networks begins with the following considerations: quality of the network, maintaining connections, investing in others, promoting diversity, time management, and thinking long term.

Quality over Quantity: Having the right people in your network is far more important than having the most amount of people in your network. If you start collecting contacts to add to your total count, they have no meaning and therefore no value.

Maintaining Connections: Don't just reach out to your contacts when you need something; take the time to reach out throughout the year when opportunities present themselves like sending congratulations for a promotion, recognizing their accomplishments, and noting important milestones in their lives: birthdays, anniversaries, retirements, or other celebrations, like the high school or college graduation of their child.

Investing in Others: Take the time to get to know who people are on a personal level, what they value, what they need, and who they know. Gaining access to their networks is how we expand ours. Being sincerely interested in their challenges and helping to solve their problems is how we maintain those contacts.

Diversity Matters: Diversified networks are stronger because they provide a mix of influencers from various fields and industries, offering a greater degree of experience, knowledge, and expertise. Assembling a network of people that only do what you do, and think the way you think, does nothing more than increase the number of people that exchange the same set of skills, thought, and experiences. It weakens our exploration of alternatives when seeking creative solutions to complex issues. Key influencers within your field are a must for any network; however, without adding influencers from outside of your field, it will never strengthen, and your knowledge to solve will weaken.

Time Management: Time is a precious commodity that is limited and while it seems we never have enough of it, we all have the same twenty-four hours in each day. Our days are filled with individual commitments and the desire to strike the perfect work/life balance that includes career, family, friends, and fun. Mastering the clock is something that comes down to time management, effectively utilizing each minute of every day by devoting those minutes to the things we value.

When it comes to servicing our networks, think about downtime opportunities like commuting to reach out and chat or check on a colleague, friend, or family member. For those living in different time zones, be considerate of their schedules and take advantage of the best times to contact them, for instance, reaching out after a late meeting on the east coast to someone on the west coast whereas a morning call from the west coast will be better received on the east coast.

Think Long Term: Connections in a network are beneficial relationships built on trust, confidence, and mutual respect. Avoid pressuring someone in your network for help or support that they're not prepared or authorized to give. Show them the same degree of respect, trust, and honor you expect or they will become short-lived. Whenever you lose a connection due to a bad break in the relationship, it carries the possibility of harming other relationships in your network as word of the mistreatment spreads. Reputation is still of paramount importance in the workplace and something every leader needs to guard at all times. To keep your networks strong, you need to ensure your connections see you as a leader possessing honor, integrity, and value. Anything less and you will find yourself losing connections and losing influence.

Now that we have addressed considerations for making beneficial connections, let's look at the second fundamental in exploring ways to achieve stronger networks. They include: utilizing social networking sites, active participation in professional associations, working the room, accessing presentation opportunities, writing articles, and community involvement.

Social Networking: Facebook, Instagram, Twitter, LinkedIn, and WhatsApp are five top apps available to help you develop and grow your network. When you consider the current crisis facing all of us with the COVID-19 closures and stay-at-home directives issued by many state governors, we remain connected to our contacts through social media, e-mails, and video conferencing. In doing so, we rely on our networks to conduct the business of remotely monitoring and conducting meetings that affect our operations through status updates and news media briefings. Even in this scenario we have the opportunity to gain new contacts.

"Now more than ever, we need to reach out to people we don't know; to find human connection in a world that seems intent on keeping us apart."[2]

Active Participation: Becoming active in professional associations ensures you are keeping pace with industry guidelines, legislation, certification standards, and best practices through quality professional development designed specifically to meet your group's needs. Associations are always looking for volunteers to be on committees, and serve as officers. These are golden opportunities to gain backstage access to directors, other officers, and trustees of those organizations. Besides providing quality programs, services, and professional growth opportunities, these associations allow access to global networks by meeting other members from various regions and states. State and national conferences are a mecca for networking.

Working the Room: The art of "working the room" is a learned skill that pays dividends in creating stronger networks. When preparing for workshops, presentations, or lectures, a good tip for successful networking is to study the list of attendees before arriving. Try to make the connections of attendees to their job titles, their organization, and the responsibilities they have within those organizations. Consider what level they are at within those organizations and how that designation can pay off down the road when you find yourself stuck trying to solve problems experienced at their level. A director, for instance, is probably not the person you want to reach out to for a detailed technical issue you are having trouble with; whereas, their assistant probably has the solution to your problem on speed dial.

When signing in at workshops, take a look through the packets provided for a list of attendees, or absent such a list upload the meeting app for the program to see if that information is provided. Getting a jump on who's who, and what they do, will pave the way to embedding them in your long-term memory.

Another trick to succeeding in networking if you're just starting is to scan the room for people you know and see who they are talking with, to gain access to conversations. Joining a conversation with someone you know is a good way to get an introduction to someone you don't. Reading name tags and making mental notes of who they are increases your chances of remembering them in future encounters. This allows you to strike up a conversation with a familiarity that produces a positive response, allowing you to engage in a meaningful conversation, and, most importantly, make a new connection. By putting a face with a name, you have created a visual link that will help your recall the next time you come in contact with that person.

Presentation Opportunities: Exploring and taking advantage of presentation opportunities allows us a quick opening to get in front of scores of potential connections. By presenting, you demonstrate your knowledge and attract more people to your network by sharing your skills and interest in areas that you have mastered. Workshops and conferences are gold mines for prospects. The best way to seize those opportunities is to plan ahead and jot down ideas based on actions or goals you successfully employed or reached, and that you believe would resonate with colleagues. Sharing your knowledge allows you to learn as you prepare, research, and present. Like anything, the more times you do this the better you will become at it, eventually mastering the skills necessary to become a highly sought-after commodity, which in turn continues to grow your networks.

Writing: Writing is a fast way to get your name out there and make connections with readers by sharing your expertise on subject matters that others may benefit from, comment on, and become followers. Blogs, newsletters, and magazines are a wonderful tool to exchange thoughts, share ideas, and link to others who struggle with the same challenges across various industries. This allows for better problem-solving through best practices.

Consider writing an article for a magazine or submitting a piece through your association's newsletter. Editors are always looking for fresh new articles from professionals and practitioners on a myriad of topics. Best tip—go on the magazine's website and locate the editorial calendar to get an advantage by knowing what the magazine's focus is on for upcoming issues and when the due dates are to ensure you are writing about topics they are looking to publish. That increases your odds of being published, versus submitting articles that, although may be well written, are just not timely or relevant.

Community Involvement: Get out into your community and get involved. Volunteerism pays dividends in many ways that enrich the lives of others, yet at the same time allows us to meet influential opinion makers and grow our networks. Serving on local boards, joining civic groups and organized clubs, coaching, and community service are all rewarding ways to expand your networks by sharing your talents while making new connections.

Beyond these two basic fundamentals, we need to focus on connectors, people within our network who belong to other networks. These connectors allow access to their networks, thus creating larger networks and widening our reach. Each time we talk to others beyond mere conversations about the weather, we begin to learn about them and understand the potential value they have in our networks now or in the future. Going back to "the more you know," in this case we are talking about people and not just random people but people in our lives. There are benefits in knowing individuals in our line of work, field of study, or area of expertise—this is the point of building a network and knowing who is suited to address the need(s) or solve the problem(s) confronting us. As our networks grow, we need to be able to recall individuals quickly and remember their strengths and skills to find the perfect match for our particular need. That's why the popularity of LinkedIn has replaced business cards with an electronic Rolodex that puts contacts just a click away.

But more important than just collecting contacts, we need to personally engage with those contacts to keep them real. Business relationships are not much different than personal relationships in as far as they need to be *managed*, *sincere*, *respected*, and *trusted*. People do not want to be used or abused even at the cost of making a sale—I have had many conversations over the years with sales people who talk about *the client they walked away from* or *the attorney who chose not to represent a particular client* or *an architect who will never work with a particular client again*. The bottom line—we build better relationships and stronger networks when we treat others the way we want to be treated ourselves—even in business.

We build business networks for a reason and it's all about knowing the right person or group in your time of need—when you see them as the solution to the problem you are working to solve. In some cases, you need many individuals or companies to forge a temporary partnership, consortium, or joint venture. Having access to a larger network will streamline the process of finding out who is capable and available especially in a pinch, when you have to have an answer yesterday, or one of your presenters just canceled and your workshop is tomorrow.

Just remember you are also in their network and it goes both ways. If you constantly reach out to people in your network for who they are and how they can help you but continuously turn them away when they request assistance from you, you are not networking—you are using, and they will stop returning you calls, and drop you from their network.

"Networking is the single most powerful marketing tactic to accelerate and sustain success for any individual or organization!"[3]—Adam Small

Diane Darling, founder and CEO of Effective Networking, Inc., and expert on the topic of networking, explains, "The real definition of networking to me is building relationships before you need them."[4]

Trying to build a network in the middle of a crisis doesn't work; at that point, you either have the connections you need or simply muddle through as best you can. Connections become the difference maker; they allow us to benefit from the strength of an ad-hoc team by assembling those who possess the skills we need at the time we need them.

A classic example to illustrate the point is the comparison of networks between Samuel Dawes (unknown) and Paul Revere (famous) in the infamous midnight ride that started in Boston on the evening of April 18, 1775. Both men played a vital role in alerting Sam Adams and John Hancock to the impending danger headed their way. While one of these men, Revere, was made famous, the other is scarcely recognized. The question is why? They both carried the same message and both equally alerted town folks, and those scattered throughout the countryside, that the British were coming.

Dawes heading south out of Boston that night rode three and half hours compared to Revere, who started about an hour after Dawes heading north out of Boston, eventually meeting up with Dawes at the Hancock-Clarke House just outside of Lexington in two hours. The difference, as pointed out in the Harvard Business Review (December 2005), was the type of social network each of them had cultivated.[5]

Gladwell refers to it as the value of social interconnectivity calling Revere a "connector" in his compelling book, *The Tipping Point*.[6] He details how Revere had already accomplished the task of cultivating an extensive network of contacts that put him right at the heart of those connections that paid off that night. Revere not only knew who the opinion makers were but also who the leaders of the local militia in each town were and where they lived, allowing him to knock on the right doors and reach the right people to spread his message.

While the final message delivered to Adams and Hancock that night actually came from a third rider, Dr. Samuel Prescott,[7] it is Revere who had the greatest impact due to his relevant network that carried the night.

The takeaway—we need to examine our networks and look at improving our connections to increase the value of those networks and ensure they are in place and ready to assist with our ability to solve problems as they surface.

Chapter 7

Empowering Leaders at Every Level

Rigidity is the enemy of problem-solving—it is the opposite of flexibility. When we become rigid in our thought process, we begin to lay the groundwork for mediocrity—turning out solutions that are just "ok" or temporary fixes (band-aids) that only mask the problem(s) we face. "Just OK Is Not OK"—AT&T built a whole ad campaign around this concept. The concept caught on quickly with funny spots featuring some of the most ridiculous compromises individuals faced in situations where "Just Ok" doesn't cut it. Adweek, a leading source of news and insight for brand marketing, featured the "Just Ok" tattoo artist as the ad of the day on January 2, 2019; it would be the first of many.[1] This clever ad campaign joining a simple concept with a wireless carrier's ability to provide exceptional service was launched by the creative talent at Batten, Barton, Durstine & Osborn (BBDO) headquartered in New York City. Not only are the spots clever and funny, they also resonate because as consumers, we don't want to settle—as leaders we should not settle. "Ok" doesn't cut the mustard when we need to find solutions that are exceptional—those that go beyond "ok" and produce results that are amazing. Settling kills creativity and extinguishes morale. That's how ideas die, and we continue to end up with solutions rooted in the concept of "past practice"— they are limited in their ability to address the problem(s) and often fall short in accomplishing measurable or effective results—they are just "ok."

So how do we break the cycle or fix the problem? Through empowerment by empowering your team with professional development, mentoring, and coaching. Start by developing your teams to become critical thinkers, creative communicators, computational thinkers, and innovative designers. This includes everyone on the team, not just those in leadership positions. By recognizing talent within the organization and providing opportunities to grow that talent, we cultivate loyalty and stimulate desire and drive. It's the stuff dreams are made of from the mailroom to the boardroom or as simple as bringing an administrative assistant to a power lunch, professional training, or workshop. When we include staff in leadership discussions and opportunities, we begin to empower them in the same way we develop interns. Exposure to the higher ups, outside professionals, and industry leaders allows those members of our team to get more involved in the process and it underscores the fact that we are invested in their future and convey a sense of worth in them individually. This stokes the fires of determination, motivation, and commitment that will more often than not generate higher returns on the investment in the form of higher productivity and engagement.

A quick lesson in human behavior or "common sense"—when you're interested in someone, they are more apt to become interested in you; if they were already interested in you and you show interest in them, now they're all in and ready to do more for you. Likewise, if you show little to no interest in them or their future, they are leaving—they are gone. Worse yet is when they lose interest but stay anyway—that is the worst outcome and far too often a fate that befalls mediocre companies that retain workers that are just "ok."

Evaluation forms that contain "Satisfactory" on their performance scale are ineffective and harmful to any organization's desire to improve performance. Satisfactory is the detrimental performance indicator for any organization as it justifies the "ok" approach to management. Ever tried terminating an employee for *satisfactory performance*, let alone a civil servant or tenured employee?—good luck! Satisfactory is the epitome of "just ok"; it sets the bar at basic level and informs the employee that while they may not be exceptional, they are *ok* and therefore safe from termination as they just received a passing grade on their performance test. Keeping these individuals on board and continuing to reward par performance with the same raises afforded to others in the group is poor management and serves to weaken the team.

While certain high performers will continue to reach higher and exceed the standards regardless of the lack of effort displayed by some, we run the risk of having others who perform well begin to slack as they move toward the lower bar of satisfactory performance, realizing the same benefit or reward with far less effort.

Why the difference within this group of high performers? Because those who remain strong and continue to strive for success are driven by integrity, pride in their work, and personal commitment to the ideals of the organization. They are the ones who want to be there, they are the ones who want to succeed, they are the ones who possess the "right stuff." These are the leaders within the rank and file that you want to build your team around. They are the individuals you should be tapping for future advancement if they so desire to move up; not everyone wants to lead, but either way these are the ones you need to keep. Top performers within any organization need to be valued through your commitment to professional development, leadership opportunity, and competitive compensation through wages and benefits. Salary guides are even worse as they offer no opportunity to reward the high achievers and continue to advance those who are average.

While the challenge of working with union-contracted employees or within organizations that regulate compensation through salary guides makes the problem of motivating staff to perform above adequacy harder, it is not impossible.

Good leaders lead—great leaders inspire! Inspirational leadership moves individuals beyond ordinary effort and allows contributions to flow from a sense of team, success, and pride—not payment. Yes, people want to get paid, people need to earn money, and higher wages are always sought; however, people want to be valued and more important they want to contribute in a way that makes them feel important. That's the difference between a job and a career.

I make a habit of bringing my team together and explaining the big picture on a monthly basis by giving an overview of current events, requirements, and any new direction on our vision quest. At the same time, it provides an opportunity for each member of the team to provide updates on their progress, discuss concerns over open issues, and have an opportunity to suggest better ways of accomplishing our mission.

Not only is that empowerment, it's smart management. They are now engaged, informed, and interested in contributing versus just "doing" their job. That style of leadership needs to carry through the entire organization, not just your own department but all departments within the organization. This is what great leaders do—they extend themselves and their abilities to other groups within the organization and welcome ideas, questions, and comments from others as well.

In our case, that means every building in the district including other departments within the administrative offices and those in our schools. By sharing our knowledge, by modeling expectations, coaching, and mentoring, we extend ourselves and our time to invest in others within the organization to ensure they succeed in their roles and ultimately allow for greater success as a district. As part of the whole, this allows me and other leaders to accomplish the mission and produce better results. When everyone is invested, we as a team not only perform well but in many cases outperform our peer groups (other high-performing districts), thus increasing our rank and benefit to the community we serve—this is how you benefit the community you serve.

Inspiration unlocks creativity and allows teams to gain a sense of ability to accomplish big things, things that without it would never be noteworthy. Leaders who have the ability to inspire achieve more from the team than those who simply manage. By inspiring those around us to actively participate in problem-solving, we create desire to achieve more and solve bigger problems. As organizations continue to raise the bar, it is often the one factor that leads to success. Absent desire, individuals have little to no drive to push the boundaries of what they feel they are capable of doing; however, great companies or organizations seem to find a way to do just that and trust me it's a team effort that begins with inspiration coupled with determination and drive. These are the companies that continue to rank high as "best places to work" and enjoy lower turnover.

Glassdoor, an Internet job search engine company, realizes that connection between the *desire to be somewhere* and *achieving success*, which serves as the cornerstone of their mission: "Helping individuals find a job and company they love."[2] In their latest annual 100 Best Places to Work ranking, covering more than 55 million employee reviews for over 1 million companies on the jobs site, they reported two key stats that employers should consider:

- 86 percent of candidates are likely to research company reviews and ratings before applying.
- 65 percent of Glassdoor users read at least five reviews before forming an opinion of a company.

Inspiring others within the organization to do more begins with fostering an environment of *why*—"whether individuals or organizations, we follow those who lead not because we have to, but because we want to. We follow those who lead not for them, but for ourselves."[3]

Growing up, we all learn from explanations of *why* versus constant commands or directives to do things, the *what*—tasks, requirements, or actions, and the *how*—steps in the process. Absent the explanation, the process is limited as we know what we need to do but now why we are doing it. If we just do it because we are told, directed, or ordered, we lose the value of learning the benefit of why we are doing it. Without the explanation of *why* we are doing an action, that action becomes just an activity that we do and repeat as necessary. Like brushing our teeth or changing the oil in our car, it leads to monotonous repetition that we begin to detest. After a trip to the dentist and the discovery of cavities from poor brushing or lack of flossing, we appreciate the need to do this task and start taking it more seriously. Perhaps we should have started at the dentist prior to learning the importance of brushing. A similar understanding of regular oil changes is learned once we get the bill from the mechanic regarding engine damage.

Tasks in our daily jobs are no exception from preventative maintenance to maintaining databases, processing reports, or managing files. The information we possess, process, and work with informs our decisions and provides knowledge available to solve problems we encounter today as well as those on the horizon of tomorrow. Take the popular trend of data mining in connection with problem-solving. Data-driven decisions require data or there is no basis for the decision as it is absent of fact-based evidence or quantifiable support. That data are inputted, managed, and stored every day through small, repetitive, and seemingly unimportant tasks; however, without the important work of those data managers, we would have nothing to mine.

Growth through professional development, research, and experience allows to get better at it and obtain a growth mindset that frees us to become clever, agile, and stronger in our thinking. When we allow the entire team to develop this skill set, we become unstoppable increasing both our ability to take on larger problems and find greater solutions. The strength of the team is what carries companies and organizations across the finish line where individuals would burn out and quit the race.

In order to consider viable solutions, we need to generate creative responses to the issues that confront us. A free exchange of ideas and thoughts designed to achieve better outcomes is what is needed to take our problem-solving skills to the next level.

In business, growth and prosperity are key to success and longevity. In education, we focus on growth with Student Growth Objectives (SGOs) to not only measure growth but also verify that it is being achieved. That it, "growth" is evident and we, "the district" are capable of delivering that expectation in a manner that is better than just ok—it needs to be exceptional in order to exceed the standards set forth by the state, the U.S. Department of Education, and the expectations of the communities we serve.

As individuals and leaders, we have choice in everything we do from the way we pursue opportunities to the way in which we deal with challenges. Great school districts, like "great companies" referred to by Jim Collins in his book *Good to Great*,[4] share many of the same attributes:

- *They don't "motivate" people—their people are self-motivated.*
- *Fear doesn't drive change—but it does perpetuate mediocrity.*
- *Dramatic results do not come from dramatic process.*
- *A down-to-earth, pragmatic, committed-to-excellence process—a framework— kept each company, its leaders, and its people on track for the long haul.*
- *Victory of steadfast discipline over the quick fix.*
- *Transformations don't happen overnight—they grow.*
- *Building tangible evidence that their plans made sense and would deliver results.*

The takeaway is simple—real success, lasting success, the kind of success that builds recognition within an industry takes time, focus, and dedication but it requires shared values and a commitment to excellence by all involved—not just the leadership. This kind of positive atmosphere is one in which leaders can be found at all levels, top-level or senior management, middle-level managers, and first-level supervisors, all of which have authority, autonomy, and support or back up. They are free to manage, lead, and make mistakes as well as taking risks. Again, reality and common sense dictate those risks and/or mistakes must be grounded in reality. Nobody is going to get a pass on recklessness or blatant disregard for the company, the organization, or its treatment of the people.

You do not have to be in a leadership role to be a leader. Anyone can step up at any time and offer leadership in helping to problem solve, which underscores their commitment to the organization. Likewise, it allows management to tap into a pool of potential individuals for advancement within that organization. What it means, what it needs to be effective, is the kind of support, encouragement, and latitude to empower those within the organization to contribute in ways that make them invested in the organization's success. This was the case a few years back with one of our building custodians who stepped up to offer a skill set way beyond the responsibilities of his job description.

Case in point—precision-drafted emergency egress plans:

Each day thousands of people rely on emergency evacuation diagrams for egress and fire safety instructions while visiting schools, office buildings, hospitals, or hotels. Basically providing a quick map of the exits and how to get to them quickly. In an emergency, they become vital as demonstrated in the explosive, action-packed blockbuster, *The Bourne Identity*,[5] when Jason Bourne grabs the evacuation sign off the wall in the embassy in Zurich to find a way out in a matter of minutes.

These documents are critical in properly addressing evacuation in the event of an emergency especially in buildings one is not familiar with such as guests in hotels or visitors to our schools. The posting of building evacuation plans, fire evacuation maps, and emergency exit signs is necessary to meet fire and building code requirements and therefore not optional but required.

Our emergency evacuation plans were basic, nondescriptive, and lacking uniformity. Every school in district had a different style, numbering system, and legend. This problem while it seems easy enough to solve required coordination with multiple architects as renovations had taken place over the years with rooms being moved and repurposed but not adjusted or updated on the exit route diagrams. To add to the confusion, principals had renumbered rooms over the year without referring to the floor plans. Building plans were scattered over multiple offices and building and in some cases missing. Bottom line, it was a mess and the plans on the walls did not accurately reflect the use, location, or room number. Attempts to solve the problem all ended the same way; those who attempted it quickly gave up and the problem was pushed aside until the next volunteer or draftee stepped forward—the cycle continued many times over a ten-year period.

Then one day one of our head custodians who had taken the initiative to redo his own school's emergency egress plan stepped forward and offered to do the same quality design work for all the schools in the district. Better still, he provided the plans in a format that made them accessible to adjustments moving forward solving another problem we often encountered with architectural plans created with AutoCAD programs we did not have access to.

Empowering leadership among the ranks of our custodians produced the passion, drive, and determination to solve a problem that we had not succeeded at solving with professionals. Instead of stifling that energy and desire to contribute, we fostered it and provided a culture where he felt valued. As a result, we gained a quality product and his connection with the district improved—he was inspired and we were the benefactors. Pursing better opportunities on his career path, he left the district a couple of years later; however, this is the first item listed on his LinkedIn profile noting the importance to him and the pride he took from completing the task for the sake of sharing his talents.

Re-designed emergency exit route plans. The emergency exit route plans were inaccurate, incomplete, and inconsistent in multiple schools due to age and new construction. Re-designed the exit routes so the perspective while looking at them was correct in relation to the actual location in the building increasing safety awareness and capabilities of staff and students.

Part 3

IMPLEMENTING SOLUTIONS

Chapter 8

The Role of Communications

Today it's not enough just to solve our problems—we need to effectively communicate the solution and the steps taken during the process. With transparency becoming an increased expectation among our stakeholders and the general public added with the "speed of the media" in reporting, companies and organizations need to have the ability to execute and deliver in "real time" with a message that resonates confidence, competence, and care.

The first known use of the word "communicate" traces back to 1529[1] derived from the Latin "communicatus," past participle of communicare, which means to share or to make common.[2] There are two basic elements of communications that are required for success—*understanding* and *sharing*. While *sharing* is the main objective of the sender in messaging with a desire to ensure *understanding* on the end of the receiver, the sender must ensure they have a firm and complete understanding of the message they are attempting to communicate.

This is true of any organization at any time—however, even more critical in the face of a crisis when emotions are high and perspective is vulnerable to tunnel vision. While the details need to be in the "now" and based on "immediate facts," it is easier to prepare general messages (templates for scenarios) prior to a crisis as you remove the "emotional" element. During the crisis, you simply review and tweak the message to include the pertinent facts that are specific to the situation. They can be in the form of a Status Report Template detailing the time, place, issue, and resolution or Incident Report recording what took place, when it took place, damage report if any, injuries if any, and the steps taken to deal with the incident. These simple suggestions help prepare any leader who is responsible for people, equipment, and buildings or departments.

This realism was decisively evidenced in response to the number of press conferences held by various state governors[3] and daily press briefings by President Trump and Governor Cuomo responding to the coronavirus outbreak,[4] the president with respect to the global crisis and its growing impact across the country and Governor Cuomo with respect to the tragic impact on and around New York City, which quickly became a major "hot spot" in March of 2020. Cuomo was praised by many for his quickness in launching a daily dialog with the people of the Empire State: "A day after New York reported its first case of novel coronavirus, Gov. Andrew Cuomo delivered words of confidence to residents."[5]

In contrast, by delaying we only weaken our position as leaders as our message gets compromised by allegations of a lack of transparency combined with criticisms including but not limited to a lack of competency, uncaring, and poor management regardless of the situation in question.

Politicians know this well as it usually manifests itself in low approval ratings from various polls. While business leaders are not necessarily associated with national polls or steady press coverage, they too are answerable to stakeholders and just as such come under scrutiny for how and when they react to any crisis and, more importantly, how they communicate their plan to handle the crisis.

I once observed key administrators spend four days crafting and drafting a response to a community issue that dragged out over several weeks before the message was finally delivered to the public. At that point, the message was marginalized and meaningless as it was preceded by multiple messages from members of the community via social media (Facebook, Twitter, and Instagram) along with a growing segment of an opposition party that mobilized and created an online petition to garner support for their position in the thousands. The takeaway—get your message right first, then get it out first.

For communications to be effective, it must be grounded in the **3 Cs**— *Confidence, Competence,* and *Care*.

Confidence: Once a message is perceived by the intended target group as being authentic, it provides the confidence and trust necessary to have believability. This is only possible when the originator, in this case the organization through its leadership, is considered to be competent. This doesn't mean things never go wrong or as planned—it just means that when you are out in front of the issue and responding to the concern(s), you are seen as capable of solving the problem(s).

At no time in recent history have we witnessed the need for leadership as a country since 9/11 with viewership at an all-time high for daily briefings on the corona pandemic. "It's the very definition of must-see television. Americans are tuned in, many are worried and looking for answers at a time of widespread uncertainty, regardless of whether they like the president or hate him." The degree of confidence in which the president speaks has a lot to do with the team of highly respected and talented professionals he assembled, "Vice President Mike Pence is in charge of the Trump administration's response to the coronavirus. But so is Deborah Birx, the physician and diplomat who the Trump administration brought on as its response 'coordinator.' Then there's health secretary Alex Azar, the chair of the Trump Administration's Coronavirus Task Force. And of course, Anthony Fauci, the director of the National Institute of Allergy and Infectious Diseases, to whom they all seem to defer."[6] With the health and safety of *America First*, the team is also staffed with those whose job it is to focus on the health and safety of the economy—a close second.

At the heart of any business crisis, we find the *Money Man* or in this case, Steven Mnuchin, treasury secretary—"instrumental in architecting a series of agreements between Trump, Senate Majority Leader Mitch McConnell (R-Ky.), and House Speaker Nancy Pelosi (D-Calif.) to provide for free coronavirus testing; financial relief for Americans who've been laid off as businesses shutter; and stabilization measures for a nosediving stock market."[7] Add former financial analyst and television financial news host Larry Kudlow, the current director of the U.S. National Economic Council, and you have the confidence of a prize fighter with a right and left to defeat COVID-19's impact on the economy.

This serves as an example of effective team building in a crisis to problem solve in a way that exudes confidence in the stakeholders you are answerable to—in this case the country. It underscores a basic tenet of smart leadership featured in *Success Magazine* (2016)—*Why Smart People Surround Themselves with Smarter People*.[8]

> Weaknesses aren't a bad thing. Recognize your shortcomings and what you need help with. Gain enough contextual knowledge to be credible and seek out others to fill in the gaps.[9]

By working with various leaders in every aspect of the crisis from epidemiology to health care, pharmaceuticals, manufacturing, logistics, and retail to finance, government, and governors, Donald Trump has put the advice into practice and as a result taken the podium each day with confidence backed by the incredible team he built.

As leaders we need to gather unto us those who possess the things we need to be better and ensure they are rewarded in ways to make them feel valued, respected, and appreciated in the ways they seek. It is not always about money, even though compensation plays a major role in attracting and retaining star performers. In times of crisis, many if not most look to share their talent, skill, and abilities to help the greater good and achieve the unthinkable to solve the problem.

"You never let a serious crisis go to waste. And what I mean by that it's an opportunity to do things you think you could not do before."

—Rahm Emanuel[10]

Confidence begins the dialog in a way that allays our fears, concerns, or discomfort. It is the central ingredient to inspire others to listen and heed the advice or accept the message as real, informed, and appropriate. Charismatic leaders have extraordinary skills in communication—they are positive, collaborative, determined, creative, and possess a vision for an improved future.

In contrast, poor leaders feed the fear and fuel anxiety during times of crises when fear is high and people are looking for encouragement. One colleague reported that her superintendent's daily update was one of negativity and stress highlighting how bad things were by sharing dramatic headlines regarding the death toll and isolated stories of individuals outside of the "high-risk group" who contracted the disease. By the end of the first week, the contact time was reduced to once a week via Zoom and an occasional letter commending the efforts of the brave staff and exceptional teachers who carried out the mission in a time of devastation.

Confidence is the calming factor in a crisis where people already grasp the reality that things are bad; without it, they go from bad to worse and if not possessed by those in charge some will sink into despair. Let your message in a time of crisis be honest, concerned, and confident in recognition of the challenges we face yet at the same time looking for and focusing on positives—promoting encouragement instead of doom and gloom. The constant ups and downs of an emotional roller coaster are difficult and exhaustive. Beyond fear lies despair, the point at which hopelessness takes root and help seems unobtainable. As leaders we cannot allow this to take hold in our people during any crisis. Despair is costly in terms of mental health, economic health, and, in the extreme, loss of life through suicide or giving up the will to live. Make no mistake, you're still going to go through the difficult period; the results however will often be better as many of those who could've lost heart, lost hope, or just quit will now fight to get through and make it.

Crises are what give us our best leaders as we see those among us who emerge as heroes creating a rally effect and guiding whole civilizations through the difficulties that hours and days before seemed unwinnable. History is ripe with examples of these type of leaders; one who jumps out is Winston Churchill—during a dark and desperate time for Londoners with the daily bombings by the German Luftwaffe during World War II, he found the courage for the people by sharing his confidence that London and bigger yet Great Britain would withstand any attack and come out of the darkness into the light.

This happens often in the consumer market with manufacturer recalls ranging from the foods we buy to the vehicles we purchase. It is when the message comes too late or is perceived to mask the real problem that confidence wanes and trust is broken. "No company likes to recall one of its products, but when a safety problem makes a product recall necessary to prevent injuries and save lives, it benefits everyone to move quickly and effectively."[11]

Competence: How we respond is how we are judged. Do we provide accurate information that explains exactly what the issue is and what we need to do to resolve that issue? Generalities are not only unhelpful at this juncture, they also beg more questions and put individual fears and concerns at risk of growing and spreading. We need to level with individuals on a large scale. What are we talking about? Be specific. By identifying the specific issues or class of individuals affected for instance, we narrow the message and limit the amount of confusion, fear, or anguish in the example of an automotive recall for a particular brand. Similar in the food industry, if you hear a message on the radio about tainted lettuce linked to *E. coli*, the immediate question is what are we talking about, red leaf, green leaf, iceberg, baby arugula, and so on? What brand? What timeline are we talking about? Does this mean all product produced by this brand or just product sold at certain locations? We need to be specific to provide real information that is worthy of dissemination.

In every business, we become aware of potential issues that are specific to our industry and organization such as funding and budgetary constraints in education, delays and changes in construction, and costs and transparency in health care. Today other challenges have become ubiquitous in all industries and are categorized by seven categories of crisis: operational, technological, humanitarian, financial, legal, human capital, and reputation.[12] These categories are not mutually exclusive—for example, a crisis of reputation can be linked directly to financial and even legal, which in some cases begins a domino effect that ends with reputation as in the case of a claim of reputation damage. While it may start in the category of legal with "reputation harm," a claim is made where a business asserts that they have suffered a loss as a result of what was said by a specific party about them. It might include things like libel, slander, or advertising injury. This can lead to either a costly settlement or judgment with a potential large payout that becomes a financial crisis, especially if your organization's liability insurance lacks adequate levels of coverage or is absent personal injury insurance.

Events are mutually exclusive if the occurrence of one event excludes the occurrence of the other(s). Mutually exclusive events cannot happen at the same time. When it comes to crisis, we often find the categories are inextricable linked and as such expands the damage on multiple fronts. Problem-solving thus becomes more critical, requiring comprehensive action steps to mitigate, resolve, and recover. This is predicated on strong crisis management plans that must be created in advance to the degree of "what if scenario(s)" developed on a broad basis to template potential actions that can be adapted and refined based on the actual circumstances in order to fine-tune the plan to fit the crisis. Thus, by creating the framework in advance of the crisis, we shorten the response time and accelerate delivery of the plan and our ability to begin messaging.

By providing a baseline that allows us to pivot while we react to a changing environment, circumstance, or event, we demonstrate the competence expected by our stakeholders and maintain the trust in our abilities to deal with major issues.

You cannot plan as effectively in the middle of a crisis—at that point, you are simply grasping to get the baseline that could now leave you scrambling to play catch up. While you still have the ability to recover, it just makes it that much harder and undoubtable longer.

Recently, we had the opportunity as many school districts and businesses across the globe to demonstrate this practice in preparation of the coronavirus disease 2019 (COVID-19).[13] What was striking were the questions that surfaced from administrators and the answers that followed from others who had already executed plans regarding the questions. In many cases, it demonstrated who was leading and who was following. Districts that took the time to plan ahead were quicker to take action and more prepared with implementation of those actions from remote delivery of instruction to remote access of critical systems such as payroll, accounting, and personnel by having virtual private networks (VPNs) already installed and tested. While "necessity is the mother of invention," learning is what prepares us for anticipating and solving problems. VPNs are now getting a lot of play in the media as the spread of the coronavirus shuts down more businesses prompting "work from home" or "remote working set ups." "Web traffic spiked 20% in one week amid coronavirus shutdown, Verizon CEO says."[14]

In a week-over-week comparison, streaming demand increased 12%, Vestberg said. Web traffic climbed 20%, virtual private network, or VPN, jumped 30% and gaming skyrocketed 75%. Social media usage remained constant.

Workplaces are making employees work remote, schools have closed their doors and restrictions are in effect on nonessential establishments as operations across America have all but halted.

Network connection has become even more critical to society as the public tries to practice social distancing. Verizon has seen "moderate growth" in network data usage, but how the data is being used has "changed dramatically," Vestberg said.[15]

This is only accomplished by working toward the reality that a crisis can and may happen; however, when it does, the extent to which we are affected and suffer is linked to the degree of weakness in our planning for that crisis.

Planning is what aids us in our ability to problem solve—without good planning, the job of problem-solving is more challenging. Those problem solvers that started working on the problem before it actually hit—"shutdowns"—saw less downtime and greater access to documents, systems, and people than those who waited to find out they had a larger challenge to achieve this task remotely. Thanks to strong IT departments and leaders within those departments at various companies/organizations, managers and executives are able to maintain operations during such crisis thus shifting their focus and resources to higher-level needs.

In preplanning for any type of crisis including the need to shut down operations and work remotely, one needs to follow six basic steps to navigate potential problems:

1. Plan ahead.
2. Stay aware (vigilance).
3. Maintain critical resources (necessities for disasters).
4. Preparation—conduct emergency preparedness trainings.
5. Preserve two-way communications—interpersonal communication.
6. Maintain access to critical systems (data, information systems, technology [VPN], building automation [BAS systems], payroll).

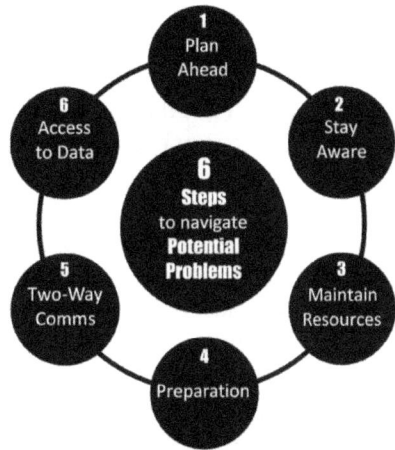

Step 1: Plan ahead—before issues happen. This is the starting point for good reason; it puts the *what-if* scenarios into action earlier and as a result, they are more effective as our planning pays off.

In the case of school closings and solving the problem of delivering education remotely, the challenge was greater for districts that lacked the resources, infrastructure, and equipment to deliver that education. The challenge to problem solve only grew as closure periods were extended.

While writing this book at the height of the crisis, more states are extending the time their schools will remain closed, some even through the rest of the school year, as the number of COVID-19 cases continues to rapidly rise. On March 24, 2020, the following article noted the growing closures:

As of Sunday, schools were closed in 46 states, according to Education Week, affecting at least 54.5 million students. Yesterday, Virginia Gov. Ralph Northam announced he will close schools in the state for the rest of the academic year, while North Carolina Gov. Roy Cooper ordered schools to remain closed through May 15. The Idaho State Board of Education, one of the few

state bodies that was leaving the decision of school closures up to local officials, has now ordered schools statewide to close until at least April 20. In the
closure order, the Board said the April 20 date could be pushed further out and
said public schools could continue to provide meals and daycare services in the
meantime. Districts will also work on developing plans for online learning. The
announcement came a short time after Idaho Gov. Brad Little said during a press
conference that he was not yet ready to make statewide or even additional local
closure orders in response to the growing number of Idaho residents confirmed
to have contracted COVID-19, the illness caused by the coronavirus.[16]

Step 2: Stay aware of your environment and what is happing in and around you.

a. Coronavirus on my radar before everyone was talking about it and raiding
   shelves at local stores—even being a week ahead makes a big difference.

Step 3: **Maintain critical resources** by keeping important things on hand.
Make sure you have the resources you may need in a crisis as they will not be
available due to supply chain breakdowns, that is, N95 masks in an outbreak,
pumps in a flood, and toilet paper in a lockdown.

b. This is different than stockpiling (outdated or dry rot) or reducing supplies
   available to others unnecessarily or putting communities at risk. In these
   events, consider transferring or donating surplus materials to those in need
   with a higher priority such as first responders in the example of masks.

Step 4: Preparation through the development of emergency preparedness
plans, scheduled drills, and continuous training. Training allows you to test
your effectiveness at dealing with potential crises and improve weaknesses
that are identified during the training. In the army, we maintained a constant
state of readiness that kept us razor-sharp and ready to answer the call—
whatever came our way.
   Quick tips for emergency drills and exercises:

• Develop emergency plans and conduct drills on a regular basis with exercises that test the organization's written emergency protocols.
• Train all employees as emergencies affect everyone and anyone can
  become a critical decision maker as situations unfold.
• Conduct tabletop exercises to plan and problem solve various scenarios
  before they are experienced in real time.

Step 5: Two-way communication—maintaining open lines of communication (internal/external) is essential in communicating actual events, impacts,
and threats. Without communications, the crisis escalates through chaos, fear,
and uncertainty to what is actually taking place.

Step 6: Access to critical systems (data, information systems, technology [VPN], BAS systems, payroll) is all needed to manage and maintain operations during any crisis.

Communication is vital to the success of any organization or company. This starts with an effective communications plan. Today's leaders need to disseminate messages that are meaningful and beneficial both internally, among staff, supervisors, and senior management, and externally, to stakeholders, community leaders, and the public. Communication strategies can be tailored to meet these contrasting needs and to cater to diverse target audiences.

Any communication strategy has a core goal: the goal of effectively getting *your organization's message* out once information is available and crafted to that aim. So, from that perspective, the *message* needs to be clear, concise, and effective—directly relating to the issue you are communicating—whether it be process, progress, or resolution. To be effective, it needs to be consumed in the quickest way possible (medium) to resonate with the understanding you wish to convey. The quickness of the exchange with the appropriate understanding is what guards against allowing others to misinterpret or mislead the narrative in a way that undermines the intent of your messaging. In plain, do NOT allow others to provide a false narrative regarding your situation or the steps that you have taken or are taking in dealing with your particular situation.

Your message, on your terms and time line, needs to be strong enough to accomplish this and correspond to your vision.

An effective communication plan needs to focus on selection of appropriate *forms of communication*—those which serve the needs of the organization relative to their audience or customer base. Social media, for instance, has grown in its use and footprint in businesses and organizations alike with continual shifts to new platforms and social networking services to drive *brand* through advertising and marketing. Instagram for one, an offshoot of Facebook, Inc., has exploded over the past few years reaching 1 billion monthly active users by mid-2018 and currently closing in on its second billion.[17] According to the report, "users post 95 million photos and videos per day, along with uploading 400 million Instagram Stories a day."[18]

"Influencer marketing is a type of marketing that focuses on using key leaders to drive your brand's message to the larger market. Rather than marketing directly to a large group of consumers, you instead inspire/hire/pay influencers to get out the word for you."[19]

To develop effective strategies, business professionals need to decide what forms of communication are most effective and what methods of delivery are most efficient. In order to control your message and drive that message, consider these helpful tips:

- *Getting out ahead of the story* before others begin to tell it by drafting key talking points that help you and others in your organization to stay on message

- *Preparing ahead of time* for journalists and reporters as not to be misquoted or ambushed by having prepared comment and quotes in advance that you want to see in the paper or online publications
- *Managing contentious meetings* by controlling the room as follows:
  - Moving the venue to a larger room and oversetting with respect to seating, anticipating a larger than expected turnout—this allows the event to appear well attended rather than overrun
  - Setting up microphones for comments in a designated place(s) to pull individuals out from the crowd when speaking—this regulates the flow of comments and limits the crowd mentality (familiarity and solidarity among friends)
  - Prepare Press Kits filled with facts surrounding the issue from the organizations' perspective along with the talking points and quotes for accuracy in reporting

Care in communications is all about how we message to ensure we get our point(s) across with the right feel when messaging to ensure those messages are on point. Messages need to be targeted based on the problem we need to solve, address, or manage. Communications without exercising care result in misunderstanding(s) and can actually do more damage requiring more problem-solving.

Whenever problems emerge, they seem big. Often we start to dig deeper into the cause and potential effect(s) and find they are even worse than first suspected or simply grow while we observe and try to figure out the best way to deal with them. This is precisely the time and opportunity to get out ahead of the problem by leveling with your superiors, stakeholders, and the public.

Often at this point in the process (discovery of an issue), leaders are simply becoming aware of the issue, having no prior knowledge or hand in creating it, but now own the responsibility for the problem. I pass this advice to mentees and key leaders by saying, "Once you become aware of it, you become responsible for it." That responsibility includes how you communicate it.

The unfortunate reality is that far too often we see leaders confronted with these type of problems trying to guard the information and solve the problem before anyone finds out about it. That is a mistake.

If left unmanaged, problems can escape our ability to deal with them and eventually grow out of control as any attempts to conceal or minimize will be seen for what they are—a cover-up. We have all heard the saying, "The cover-up is worse than the crime"—this is a perfect example of just that when officials take the fall who had nothing to do with cause of an issue. By failing to communicate the problem while attempting to solve it, they take on a tremendous amount of criticism and blame—eventually creating a real problem for themselves that leads to forced resignations or buyouts that cost those organizations even more.

Recognizing the need for communications in the aftermath of situation that evolved into a mishandled problem that became a community nightmare for one New Jersey school district leading to the resignation of a superintendent and the retirement of the school business administrator, the school board president was quoted saying, "Communication with the entire school community will be a major initiative going forward."

Chapter 9

The Courage to Solve

In ancient times, there were those who came forth with messages for the people, warnings of what was to come, and what they needed to do to change their ways—they were called prophets. The messages they carried were not always popular and many of the people did not want to hear or take heed of the news they carried as it was not in line with their thoughts or beliefs; it meant change. Today, many leaders still suffer the same effect, their ideas are labeled extreme or radical, too fast or too expensive; they are called change agents.

Sometimes finding the answer to a problem is easier than putting it into action. Solutions that address difficult problems are often unpopular and unwelcomed. Solving problems takes courage, the courage to step forward and put out solutions that at times are not well received as they can be seen by others as costly, disruptive, unnecessary, and unwelcomed especially before the problem is recognized by others. The best problem solvers are those who have the ability to foresee problems before they happen or worse become a large-scale crisis. These are *planners*, as planning is key in preparation and problem avoidance; however, even the best-laid plans encounter obstacles that need to be overcome. All organizations and leaders will be confronted with problems even if they are well prepared, due to an ever-changing set of variables they encounter. The more prepared you are to deal with problems, the more successful you will be at solving them.

David Deutsch, an award-winning pioneer in the field of quantum computation, argues that explanations have a fundamental place in the universe. They have unlimited scope and power to cause change, and the quest to improve them is the basic regulating principle not only of science but of all successful human endeavor.

> Some problems are hard, but it is a mistake to confuse hard problems with problems unlikely to be solved. Problems are soluble, and each particular evil is a

problem that can be solved. An optimistic civilization is open and not afraid to innovate, and is based on traditions of criticism. Its institutions keep improving, and the most important knowledge that they embody is knowledge of how to detect and eliminate errors.[1]

The courage to solve carries many of the same risks today that confronted the prophets of the past. When the stakes are high, when the decisions are huge, the risks are equally as dangerous for the individual as they are for the company or organizations they lead. There are many parallels regarding this risk some small and others huge, albeit potential career-ending for those who risk everything on and executive decision versus the actual end of life for many of the prophets. Foreseeable risk is a characteristic they share containing a hero (the change agent), opposition (the resistors), and courage and commitment (their belief in the cause).

Prophets were not always welcomed as their messages were not upbeat or positive; they often required the people of the time to change their ways and heed the message or warnings of what would befall them if they did not. Although this was many generations ago, and continues to be disputed today by nonbelievers with respect to authenticity, accuracy, and whether they possessed heavenly powers from God, the messages they carried were as challenged then as those espoused today by superintendents, CEOs, or top executives who say what is not always popular. The reaction remains the same—one of negativity, distrust, and denial of the messages the employees, stakeholders, or greater community do not wish to hear.

Often times the message evokes anger, irritation, and annoyance with those who deliver the news. Hence the common phrase, "Don't shoot the messenger!" This was clearly evidenced in the typical fate that befell most of the prophets in their day—the ending of their life. Among the violent deaths described in the apocryphal *Lives of the Prophets*[2] are those of Isaiah by being sawn in two, Jeremiah by stoning, and Ezekiel by a similar execution.

While stoning does not happen today and no one has been sawn in two since Jeremiah's time, leaders today require the same courage to face the public and their own stakeholders at the risk of being replaced or removed from the organizations they serve. Today's leaders need to be courageous in solving problems by putting themselves out there with messaging that may not be initially welcomed. That's why communications are so important in how you craft those messages and the need to prepare the receivers for the messages to come.

Today there are far too many companies and organizations that find themselves employing damage control over situations resulting from problems that were either mishandled or could have been avoided had they acted to solve the problems they faced at the onset. Why do they often pass on the opportunity to solve or simply kick the can down the road? Because they are not willing to champion solutions that are unpopular or difficult, even though they would be the appropriate course of action and produce better outcomes. These types of decisions should be seen as "short-term pain—long-term gain" when espousing the need to tackle these type of problems.

Han-Gwon Lung, award-winning CEO and cofounder of Tailored Ink, a copywriting and content marketing agency based in New York City, believes in this action, "I truly believe brilliant leaders should always take action, even if they're not 100% sure of the outcome. Inaction can often lead to even bigger problems."[3]

Business Insider, a fast-growing business site with deep financial, media, tech, and other industry news, published an article written by Lung in October of 2016 profiling three CEOs who saved their companies by making unpopular decisions.[4] Those individuals and the problems they faced exemplify the courage required to see the future of their decisions despite the challenges of the present and the unpopularity of taking the hard road. One of those cases that remains a classic example today of how to manage a recall was criticized by many at the time as an overreaction.

The implementation of tamperproof packaging came out of courage and vision to see a problem that existed and the potential negative impact it would have on the company's future if left unaddressed. This courageous decision serves as a classic example of how one leader defied the pushback of many to set a course for recovery and save a huge company. This is the story of Johnson & Johnson during the Tylenol poisoning in the early 1980s and their CEO James Burke.

Case in point—James E. Burke and Tylenol tampering

In 1982, contaminated Tylenol capsules resulted in 7 deaths, including that of a 12-year-old girl. In September of the same year, someone tampered with the packaging and laced the medicine with cyanide in Chicago. A month later in California, Tylenol was laced with a different poison, strychnine. Four years later, another woman died from cyanide poisoning in extra-strength Tylenol.[5]

As headline news of these horrible deaths, labeled by the press as "The Chicago Tylenol Murders,"[6] spread across the country, it evoked fear and panic resulting in immediate loss of consumer confidence in the safety of Johnson & Johnson's products.

While the situation was dire and potentially company ending for the manufacturer Johnson & Johnson, the courage to take swift and appropriate action not only saved a great company that is still around today in force, but it also earned its leader a distinguished and honored place in history for doing the right thing. "Former CEO James E. Burke's response actually earned him a Presidential Medal of Freedom from President Bill Clinton in 2000."[7]

Instead of hiding from the negative press or shifting blame, Burke got in front of the crises by:

- Recalling all Tylenol sold in October 1982
- Offering coupons to reimburse customers
- Stopping all advertising for Tylenol after the incidents
- Spreading awareness of the issue to doctors' offices, hospitals, and trade groups
- Pushing for the development of the tamperproof packaging we use today
- Discontinuing capsules after 1986 for ensured safety

When asked about the recall, Burke said that he listened and was sympathetic. "I was still very concerned that this was not the right solution, either from the point of view of the public or from the point of view of my company's business," he said.

Many considered the recall an overreaction until 75 cyanide-laced capsules were found. Johnson & Johnson suffered immediate losses of at least $100 million and a 7% drop in stock price. But they quickly recovered and regained 30% of the market. Thirty years later, Johnson & Johnson remain a trusted brand in households everywhere.[8]

Courage starts with conviction, a belief in your idea and the merits of your solution. With every decision we make as leaders, we must ask ourselves one simple question: Does it benefit the group, the company, the district, the organization? If the answer is yes, then you can voice it and champion your own cause—finding the right solution for the problem at hand and stay the course.

Tamper evidence seals and plastic shrink wrap on health and beauty products today are considered commonplace. Back in the 1980s that decision and the Tylenol recall by Johnson & Johnson cost millions for an industry that at the time held large inventories, not like the today's inventories reduced to a minimum through just-in-time (JIT) manufacturing. In the words of one packaging plant manager who worked at Schering Plough during that time, "Old J&J handled that right, despite the costs incurred, they stepped up and saved lives not to mention avoiding large lawsuits."[9]

It's never the wrong time to do the right thing and its always right time to take a stand for what is right, just, and fair.

That is leadership in action, that is being a leader people can follow, that's the kind of leader people want to follow.

Burke passed away in October of 2012 at the age of eighty-seven. A week later, *Time* magazine reported Burke had been named one of history's ten greatest CEOs by *Fortune* magazine in 2003. "But it was for his handling of the Tylenol tragedy back in 1982 that Burke, CEO of Johnson & Johnson from 1976 to 1989, will be remembered most."[10]

Every decision we make as leaders carries with it the consequences of those actions good and bad. While we always look for sure bets, we often find ourselves confronted with unknowns (variables) that will undoubtedly impact our outcomes both positive and negative. What we can control, what we always must do is stay true to our convictions and have the courage to do what we believe is right, fair, and in the best interests of those we serve.

A good friend and former board member I had the privilege to work with ends all of his e-mails with a quote from Fredrick Douglas, "If there is no struggle, there is no progress." That's powerful and fitting regarding the connection of courage to problem-solving. We cannot compromise our principles to steer clear or avoid addressing the problems that need to be dealt with. To do so is simply taking the easy way out at the expense of the future of the company or organizations that we serve.

A wise man once said, "Problems are not stop signs, they are guidelines." A wise guy on the other hand said, "Even a fish can avoid problems if it keeps its mouth shut."

Saying nothing says it's ok—this was practical advice given to me by an even wiser woman, and that is the premise behind beginning the dialog necessary to address the problems we must face. Thanks Nancy!

It takes courage to face our biggest challenges especially when the solution comes with unpleasant or ill effects for the group or person leading the charge. Courage is the quality that moves us past our fear in deciding to take action despite the risks. Look at the heroes on the front line of any crisis; they run into the fires. They put themselves at risk for the benefit of others. It's the same when we see leaders who take on the issues confronting their people and organizations regardless of the cost to themselves publically (press, media, public) or privately (family, friends). They speak out for what is right, they speak out for the group!—They are *brave*.

Sara Bareilles wrote a song about it,[11] and Disney and Pixar made a movie about it![12] Soldiers are remembered for it each Memorial Day and Veterans Day. Magical movies, Disney's specialty, are all about it because we all aspire to be brave; but without courage, it will never become reality. You have to be able to risk everything—criticism, questioning, challenges to your authority, and even ridicule. Those who fight through such challenges deliver results that are far from ordinary and some end up having their stories retold through print, music, and motion pictures.

One of the best examples of this was legendary ice hockey coach Herb Brooks hired to coach the 1980 Olympic team, which later became a Disney film, *Miracle*.[13]

Brooks had to solve a problem, how to beat the Soviets. In order to accomplish this, he had to change the way they played the game. He realized that selection of players who could work as a team, challenge as a team, and play as a team was the only way to win as a team.

Fighting criticism, second guessing, and threats of being fired by organizers and members of the 1979 Olympic Ice Hockey committee, he stuck to his plan of handpicking his team then training them to attack the game at an exhaustive pace. He did not waiver in his belief that he had the solution to the problem, refusing to back down even going against the concerns of his assistant coach Craig Patrick, stating, "I'm not looking for the best players, Craig, I'm looking for the right ones." The rest is history as they went on to win gold including victory over the seemingly invincible Soviet squad.[14]

Visionary leaders can be found throughout organizations and courage is not reserved for only those at the top. Decisions require courage on the ground and in the trenches as much as those made in the boardroom. As described in chapter 7, leadership can be found at any level and anyone in a leadership role can become an agent of change. New talent who aspire to lead the team to new heights and change the course or culture of an organization, but run the risk of being branded as zealots, are often met with strong resistance. This same phenomenon is applicable to existing leaders who dare to step forward and change course in any company, department, or district without gaining the buy-in necessary for success.

This is especially true of those who are comfortable with the status quo and have become lazy. In the military, we referred to these types as Retired on Active Duty (ROAD); the truth is they are all around us and especially prevalent in jobs that offer safety and security (protection from termination) through tenure, seniority, and union representation. This is why leaders need both courage and bravery when challenging the status quo by making changes in practice, policy, or personnel. That doesn't mean it can't be done; it just recognizes an additional hurdle or two and the need to navigate a few minefields along the way.

Change is difficult, but it is achievable. A successful change agent recognizes the opportunity for change, identifies the best approach, and makes that change happen—that is problem-solving at its best. Directing that change requires action; however, equally important is strategy to succeed in implementing the change by having a real understanding of the people and culture before you start storming through the process.

If we blindly follow the call to action (CTA) in the Sara Bareilles song Brave[15] of *saying what we want to say and letting the words fall out*, you're probably going to be looking for a new job!—*Honestly!* That's not being brave, that's being reckless with your words and your career—that's reality. Again that doesn't mean staying silent; it means thinking before you speak and organizing those thoughts into words that articulate your intent, concern, or challenge and then putting those words into action, a solution.

> "Success is not final; failure is not fatal: it is courage to continue that counts."
>
> —Winston Churchill

Recognizing the right thing is easy—doing it is what is hard. Courage to find the right words makes it possible.

Chapter 10

Controlling Our Environments

As we prepare for the "what-if" scenarios, we need to deal with the "here and now"; yet with each new challenge, such as the latest, COVID-19, our focus has shifted to more of a "what now and what's next" as the rate of change in our environments has increased faster than ever before. Staying ahead of the curve is likewise trickier than ever before requiring roadmaps for every crisis or big decision from opening our economies (regional, state, and national) to opening our schools as the curve flattens.

The surge in global demand for products like masks, gloves, and hand sanitizer during the pandemic has forced business and organizations to map out ways to acquire these products as the coronavirus pandemic disrupts and dismantles global trade. Industry cleaning companies are shifting to "sanitization experts" and the service industry that includes lodging, food and drink service, event planning, theme parks, and transportation are mapping ways to restore consumer confidence in their ability to provide environments that are safe, clean, and germ-free.

"The coronavirus pandemic is forcing us to confront weaknesses in our trade system in real time—and to improve it in time for the next major disruption."[1]

While roadmaps provide the routes for our travels, they do more than just illustrate pathways; they help get us to our destinations quicker, as they provide guidance and information along the journey. Signage guides us on that journey and warns us of the potential dangers along the way. Limited site distance signs inform us to proceed with caution since danger could be just around the corner. Yellow signs are basically a risk avoidance system with different types signifying other warnings—they help us maintain control over the road.

In business, mastering something, anything takes time, thought, and effort to gain a deep understanding and appreciation of not only how it works but also why it works and what factors could prevent it from continuing to work. It is the same for gaining control over our environments—it is a learned approach that takes time as opposed to taking control, which is quick, forceful, and domineering. As leaders, there are times we need to take control in order to deal with immediate threats to our people, our property, or our business. Although it is necessary to protect the business or organization in the short term by taking control, gaining control is how we protect our interests for the long term. When it comes to our work environments, gaining control is about heeding the warning signs, seeking continuous improvement, and seizing opportunities based on a clear understanding of those environments in which we work, coexist, and grow.

Gaining control over our environments as leaders is essential to risk avoidance, improving performance, and seizing opportunities.

It starts with being well informed—understanding what the issues are both internally (your world) and externally (the world). In order to exercise control, you need to know what's happening, what's up, and why it matters.

Information drives our decisions as they become informed, fact-based, and data-driven; without it, we are flying blind and just doing things that may be the wrong things.

The first element in gaining control over our environments deals with risk through avoidance and mitigation both responses to an overall risk response plan.

RISK AVOIDANCE (Offense) versus RISK MITIGATION (Defense)—

Avoidance is an offensive response in our planning that allows us to steer clear of risk through strategies designed to eliminate that risk whenever and wherever possible. But the reality is risk is always present and in many cases unplanned, unwelcomed, and unavoidable. As such, we need to incorporate mitigation into our planning to reduce the impact, harm, or damage that comes with such risk as is the case with cautionary road signs. Effective risk management is essential in ensuring that the risks we do encounter do not jeopardize our primary objective—carrying out our mission. By identifying the risks in our environment and assessing the probability of those risk materializing, we gain control in planning how to best avoid such risk by using the information available to aid in creating those plans and adjusting accordingly as situations change.

One example of project plan adjustment coming out of the coronavirus pandemic to avoid further disruptions in our supply chains includes changing a foreign supplier to a local one to avoid exposure to the global volatility risk experienced with China.

Mitigation is a defensive move that acts to lessen the impact and allow us to recover. Mitigation provides organizations and businesses with a form of protection against a possible risk as is the case with insurance. Mitigation is the act of reducing the severity, seriousness, or distress associated with risk. Insurance does not preclude a loss from happening, but it does protect the insured from that loss.

Likewise, testing in all forms acts as a mitigation strategy as we learn from the results of those tests where our weaknesses lie and what adjustments need to be made to avoid further risk. That is the point of diagnostics in research and development as well as student-based assessments that let us know whether our goals are being met in education. Both examples serve to underscore the importance of mitigation strategies in the learning process—what is working and what is problematic.

Assessing the cause of a risk event is an integral part of any risk mitigation strategy as we need to know what to protect against and then go back on offense—risk avoidance.

Addressing risk requires us to identify trends and develop an awareness of cause-and-effect relationships in our environments. This skill not only enables us to fix the problems we encounter; it also allows us to problem solve in a way that builds more cohesive teams that perform better with each new challenge they encounter.

The strength of the team in problem-solving stems from a Hive Mind mentality that operates through a free flow and exchange of ideas in pursuit of options that become solutions to address the risks we face. The collective is stronger and better at solving larger problems and avoidance of bad decisions or actions that would fall short of the mark in addressing those problems by a single individual. That is why we must employ strong teams and then engage them to the fullest in pursuit of gaining control over our environments.

This Hive Mind collective team concept benefits our organizations and companies as it leads to better performance and, in turn, better results. "Problem-solving can be applied to the anticipated future events and used to enable action in the present to influence the likelihood of the event occurring and/or alter the impact if the event does occur."[2]

Daily briefings are a part of any CEO's world but the benefits of being informed extends to others leaders in the Hive (the organization) and anyone preparing for a vertical climb (future leaders) as "information is power"—back to Bacon.[3]

How we obtain that information differs as mediums continue to evolve through the use and advancement of technology, providing a myriad of choices from the delivery system: print, radio, TV, or social media, to the times in which we chose to get that information. "According to a newly published Pew Research Center report 55% of U.S. adults now get their news from social media either 'often' or 'sometimes'—an 8% increase from last year. About three-in-ten (28%) said they get their news 'often,' up from 20% in 2018."[4]

So how do the busiest leaders make time to get their news information? The 2015 Quartz Global Executives Study answered just that:

> Quartz surveyed 940 executives in the top tiers of their respective organizations and from a range of industries and global regions to better understand how the world's smartest, busiest people consume news every day, source and share industry intelligence—and respond to branded content and native advertising. Do they read news in meetings, or on the way to lunch? In the restroom, perhaps? How much time do they have for consuming content, in all its flavors, anyhow? (The answer: 30–60 minutes, for 39 percent of them.)[5]

Again quality is the issue, not quantity; it doesn't have to be large segments or blocks of time committed to getting the news but rather the task should be authentic, targeted, and encompassing based on the relationship to what you are doing and how that news affects your operation.

In contrast, poor leaders operate under the premise that "ignorance is bliss" figuring what they don't know protects them from accountability. They have their head in the sand. When it comes to getting the news, they are content to be selective, focusing only on good news or limiting their intake, opting instead to cherry-pick or glean the headlines—thus skewing the *work–life balance* in favor of *life* over *work* to escape the pressures of world. This is a mistake and one that will eventually find them unprepared, reactionary, or behind the curve. They will not last and while they are occupying positions of leadership, they'll not be effective in preparing or dealing with the challenges confronting their organization, their industry, or what lies ahead.

In contrast, successful leaders who are committed to their people and their organizations wrestle with just the opposite problem, favoring *work* in their struggle to maintain the balance.

Maintaining a work–life balance helps reduce stress and prevent burnout. It keeps the creative juices flowing for top-level executives tasked with problem-solving to confront issues before they happen and deal with the unforeseen ones. By creating a work environment that prioritizes work–life balance, leaders can reenergize and maintain a more productive effort in dealing with challenges.

While work–life balance is important and critical to maintaining longevity and productivity for all within an organization, accountability must be part of the culture and enforced. If not, some leaders will abuse the concept to evade or avoid work by lessening their commitment to the organization, team, and people who are invested in them as leaders.

The "absence of presence" by a leader has a detrimental impact on morale. An absent leader has the same effect as an absent parent—one who has abandoned his or her child—in this case, the team—by failing to maintain an appropriate degree of contact. The question is how long can that behavior last? The answer: It won't. At some point, the absence will be realized by the governing body and corrective action will be enforced. However, the longer it is permitted, the deeper the damage to the organization in the form of lower productivity and morale.

Consider the viewpoint of those above or beneath these absent leaders; they equate the large salaries and benefit packages afforded these leaders with the extra time commitment expected in return. That is how individuals within an organization reconcile with what is fair and what makes sense. It maintains harmony and allows for good morale and therefore higher productivity, less absenteeism, and all the things one desires and expects from a great company or organization. It is called accountability and it should always start at the top. This is how great leaders control their work environments by modeling the behaviors, commitment, and degree of accountability they seek in others and uphold versus an empty proclamation.

Back to the news—while not always pleasant, happy, or encouraging, news is filled with information that you need to be aware of (1); process by discerning fact from fiction (2); and consider the impact if any on your business, your employees, your customers, and the larger community (3). Absent this ability to stay informed, a leader will certainly fall short in the area of controlling his or her environment as they are left simply unprepared.

Case in point: School districts in New Jersey that were planning for the *what-if* scenario of school closings in February of 2020 had a clear leg up on those who reacted to the actual orders that came out in the middle of March—Governor Murphy's Executive Order 104[6] (2020) and Executive Order 107[7] (2020).

In Summit, we got a jump on mapping a plan for delivery of remote instruction, ensuring connectivity and devices for students, providing meals for our low-income population, and maintaining our buildings during the COVID-19 closure because we were talking about it in our weekly cabinet meeting on February 25 and considering worst-case scenario should we have to close the schools.

Speaking with one colleague at that time confirmed the *Ostrich Approach* is alive and real as his chief school administrator brushed it off with the comment, "I'm not one to over react" and likened it to the H1N1 scare. A week and half later that superintendent was forced to hastily correct course and get on board but now lacked the time to plan methodically, left instead to rely on other districts such as ours who had begun to roll out action plans.

Leaders who refuse to face reality or recognize the truth place their organizations and their people in harm's way or, at the very least, at a clear disadvantage when it comes to problem-solving as they consistently find themselves up against the clock.

The item made its way to our agenda under *discussion* that day based on insights drawn from following world news stories that continued to escalate over the concern of future spread and potential lockdowns and what that would do to our overall operations and mission of providing quality instruction for our students. Those events included the following:

Feb. 4—"The Diamond Princess cruise ship was quarantined in Yokohama with about 3,700 people, including passengers and crew, onboard."[8]

Feb. 11—"The World Health Organization (WHO) announcing that the disease caused by the new coronavirus will be known by the official name of COVID-19."[9]

Feb. 20—"South Korea reporting its first coronavirus death, as the country's number of confirmed cases rose to 104."[10]

Feb. 24—"Italy becoming the worst-hit country in Europe as cases spiked leading to The U.S. stock market plummeting over coronavirus fears, after the Dow Jones Industrial Average experienced the worst day in two years."[11]

As we would find out two weeks later, we were right on target and the problem was bigger than any of us imagined at the time. We closed our schools on Friday, March 13, three days ahead of the Executive Order requiring it.

While preparing for a three-week closure to give us an extra week to clean, sanitize, and make ready for the return of students, none of us knew at the time we would not be returning for the remainder of the school year—that decision would come to us in the first week of May from the governor in a highly watched press conference.

IMPROVING PERFORMANCE—The second element of gaining control over our environments requires us to focus on improving performance. In order to accomplish this critical task, we need to know our people, our organizations, and why we do what we do. It requires a realization that we are all connected and our actions have a causal relationship on others in the organization. Those actions have either a direct impact or indirect impact on the environments we operate in, both internal (our organization) and external (our industry). Poor performance weakens the team; if left unaddressed, that weakness can spread like a cancer attacking other cells, in this case other employees who willingly or not, serve to expand the damage.

Strategies designed to improve performance include seven basic actions steps, each one a piece of the puzzle that management must assemble. Like any good puzzler knows, we begin by building the border (*edge pieces*) and working our way inward; this allows us to fill in the center working with sections. To get our *edge* for improved performance, we start by:

7 STRATEGIES FOR IMPROVED PERFORMANCE

Set clear expectations – link goals with objectives

Communicate the mission, vision and purpose

Conduct meaningful performance appraisals – consistently and honestly

Commit to strong professional development – impactful, engaging and targeted

Empower employees to act at every level – with autonomy and accountability

Outfit teams with the proper gear (supplies, equipment, technology)

Maintain high levels of morale – implementation of recognition and reward program

1. **Setting clear expectations by linking goals with objectives.** This ensures everyone understands what is expected and what the targets are. This also ties directly to #3—performance appraisals as employees need to know up front what are the standards by which they will be measured. Informing them at the end of the period is meaningless.
2. **Communicate the mission, vision, and purpose—clearly and often.** Communication makes it happen. By communicating the mission (*what we do*), the vision (*where we are going*), and the purpose (*why we do what we do*), everyone understands their role in the organization. Like a jigsaw puzzle, organizations contain different-shaped interlocking tiles (personnel) that require assembly by putting each piece where it fits best to produce the complete picture once properly assembled.
3. **Conduct meaningful performance appraisals—consistently and honestly.** Evaluations are designed to improve performance and as such should be given serious weight by both parties. It is not meant to punish, intimidate, or demean the person being reviewed, but instead should focus on what is going well, where they stand out, what they have achieved and where they need to improve. Poor performance is just as important to include and review during the evaluation as honestly as possible without the negative or hostile emotions that sometimes visit the narrative. Used properly, they are a tool to recognize outstanding effort, reiterate expectations, notice areas for improvement, and provide targets for future growth.

    When leaders begin to miss, delay, or skip evaluations, they diminish their importance and denigrate their value.
4. **Commit to strong professional development—impactful, engaging, and targeted.** Strong professional development is how we learn, stretch,

and stay engaged. Workshops and conferences have long been critical to providing quality growth as we network, share ideas and best practices, and improve our means and methods.

The planning and selection of PD opportunities should ensure they are meaningful and not just time away from our daily tasks. The best response to any training is when individuals walk away feeling energized, invigorated, and reconnected.

5. **Empower employees to act every level—with autonomy and accountability.** When we empower our employees to act, we do more than just extend authority or power to do something, we allow them to become stronger as an integral part of the team and more confident to make decisions that reduce unnecessary delays waiting for basic approvals. This hinges on trust and accountability to avoid overstepping or abuse.

6. **Outfit teams with the proper gear (supplies, equipment, technology).** Without the right equipment, setup, and supplies, we are not going far and can become frustrated with the lack of concern perceived by the employee(s). While *passion trumps resources*, reality tells us from experience the passion will die without energy. Energy levels are tied to morale—high morale-high energy, low morale-low energy. When people struggle too long to *make do* and continuously have their requests for better tools and equipment including technology to accomplish their work denied, they will stop asking and stop trying to excel. They will do what they can and call it a day!

7. **Maintain high levels of morale—implementation of recognition and reward program.** In addition to the above strategies, each having a significant role in improving and maintaining high levels of morale, it is recognition and reward that allows individuals to thrive. Being appreciated for what we do is a basic human need. "The deepest principle in human nature is the craving to be appreciated."—Psychologist William James[12]

The time, effort, and money that go into creating and maintaining strong reward systems and programs to honor those committed to the success of the organization is simply an investment that pays huge dividends in return.

These strategies are connected and as such dependent on one another to reach beyond OK and achieve greatness.

SEIZING OPPORTUNITY—In order to seize any opportunity, we must be ready, willing, and able—ready to try, ready to risk failing, and ready to try again until we get it right. The same strategies suggested above to improve performance aid in the willingness and ensure we are able to meet these challenges. It starts with perspective and mindset—the way in which we view problems and how we go about addressing them. When we shift from a negative perspective of problems to view them as opportunities, challenges that we take head-on, then we move beyond mere solving and begin focusing on improving. Seeing things not as they are but how they can become is the definition of vision. While vision is a paramount requirement for any CEO or president, vision itself is not restricted to them alone, it is once again available for all within the structure; however, their vision must align and support the larger vision that leads the organization.

When we improve something, we make it better. When we fix something, we make it work again. In order to gain control or master our environments, we need to move beyond applying quick fixes or worse prolonged costly ones. That just wastes vital resources, time, and money as we push the problem into tomorrow. We cannot just respond to the problems we face by fixing them, not if our aim is control. A fix is short term to keep things going with a quick repair—a patch, band-aid, or duct tape. Whereas improvements are long term and who wants to settle for *ok* when you can have *better*. Once we move beyond band-aids and duct tape to repair our environments, we generate fixes that improve those environments by providing solutions that are better, healthier, and lasting.

"Problem-solving isn't just about responding to (and fixing) the environment that exists today. It is also about innovating, creating new things and changing the environment to be more desirable. Problem-solving enables us to identify and exploit opportunities in the environment and exert (some level of) control over the future."[13]

Every problem situation we encounter possesses the potential for a setback or disruption in our process, our purpose, and our mission. We can simply fix the problem by addressing the cause to return to a state of readiness, the way things were or getting the operation back on track. Keeping the machinery up and running by addressing the part or element that failed. This is commonly referred to as an "in-kind" replacement by swapping out the faulty piece. It is the same with personnel when someone leaves and we simply run the same old ad that was used to fill the position when they came on board. Sometimes that is all that is needed and again common sense should rule the day and the decision process. Not every issue is a problem or needs to be reengineered; however, while we may achieve our objective in the short term, replacing the part or person, we miss the larger opportunity to improve the overall process.

Instead of restarting the production line or restaffing personnel with the same old job responsibilities, we should take the time to seize the opportunity to implement effective change by upgrading our equipment, our personnel, and our processes. When things break down, we get an immediate *fast-pass* to action as they must be fixed. Planning for such fixes in advance allows us to control our environments and shape them in a way that continues to improve our overall mission and *fast-track* our success.

I've seen it happen time and again to leaders, it has happened to me—you are up against the clock to deal with your problem whether it be mechanical systems or human resources and you end up doing what you have to in place of what you want to because you weren't prepared.

So how do we guard against this reality? By being prepared. Preparation through an understanding of our environments means investigation and researching options for the replacement of equipment, systems, and personnel in advance of the breakdown. Knowing what's out there (external) by attending trade shows, reading industry magazines, and participating in workshops and seminars allows us to ready ourselves for the challenges (internal) that come our way, and deal with them swiftly and confidently when they strike.

Controlling our environments both internal and external is achievable through an in-depth analysis and understanding of those environments and then developing strategies and plans designed to improve them.

Epilogue/Conclusion

Problem-solving today requires flexibility, creativity, and the ability to adapt to the changing environments that we face as leaders both new and seasoned alike.

Six essential skills to ensure success in meeting these standards for new leaders should include: active listening, analysis, creativity, communication, decision making, and team building.

6 Essential Problem-Solving Skills

Active Listening

Logic, sense and reason

Analysis

Analytical skills

Creativity

Flexible mindset

Communication

Clear and meaningful

Decision Making

Facts based – Data rich

Team-building

Active participation

Mastering these skills will require determination, discipline, hard work, and personal accountability.

While the focus on *new leaders* is critical to leadership development, we need to ensure *all leaders* within our organizations are actively pursuing continuous education through meaningful professional development. This includes *seasoned leaders* at the top levels who need to stay current on what's changed and what's new, rather than relying on what's happened and what's worked in the past. Likewise, we need to continue to develop future leaders in our talent pools.

As leaders, we have a clear responsibility to mentor, support, guide, and develop our future leaders to ensure the *hive* is active and ready to solve the problems that come our way.

In an ever-changing world, our environments change at a constant rate—at times fast and furious, yet others like a slow burn, but changing nonetheless. We often find ourselves in a tug of war between progress through change, pushing boundaries and challenging the status quo, and familiarity, the comfort of keeping things as they are.

The first (progress) offers the promise of success through change, seizing on the need to innovate, reengineer, retool, and reinvent to move our organizations forward. The second (familiarity) serves as a testament, a tangible proof, or tribute to the way things have always been done. The truth is we need a blend of both in order to be successful in the evolutionary change that is needed to stay on top in any industry or ahead of the curve in avoidance of problems. As stated earlier, regardless of the strategies we employ to avoid risk, problems, and/or challenges, they are ubiquitous and as such require bright creative minds to solve them.

Change impacts our environments both external and internal, whether we see it or want to see it; it happens and it is happening all the time. To deal successfully with external changes, we must master our internal environment or we are finished before we start.

Notes

CHAPTER 1

1. Friedman, Thomas L. "How to Get a Job at Google." *New York Times*, February 22, 2014. https://www.nytimes.com/2014/02/23/opinion/sunday/friedman-how-to-get-a-job-at-google.html.

2. Sundem, Garth. *Beyond IQ: Scientific Tools for Training Problem Solving, Intuition, Emotional Intelligence, Creativity, and More*. New York: Three Rivers Press, 2014.

3. Ibid.

4. Dweck, Carol. "What Having a 'Growth Mindset' Actually Means." *Harvard Business Review*, January 13, 2016. https://hbr.org/2016/01/what-having-a-growth-mindset-actually-means.

5. Merriam-Webster.com Dictionary, s.v. "expansion," accessed June 3, 2020. https://www.merriam-webster.com/dictionary/expansion.

6. Merriam-Webster.com Dictionary, s.v. "growth," accessed June 3, 2020. https://www.merriam-webster.com/dictionary/growth.

7. Randazzo, Sara. "Crumbs Bake Shop Closing Its Doors." *Wall Street Journal*. Dow Jones & Company, July 8, 2014. https://www.wsj.com/articles/sticky-time-for-crumbs-bake-shop-1404770884.

8. Wikipedia contributors. "Crumbs Bake Shop." Wikipedia, The Free Encyclopedia, accessed June 3, 2020. https://en.wikipedia.org/w/index.php?title=Crumbs_Bake_Shop&oldid=943777791.

9. DeMers, Jayson. "5 Companies That Grew Too Quickly (and What You Can Learn from Them)." *Entrepreneur*, March 12, 2018. https://www.entrepreneur.com/article/310166.

10. Peterson, Hayley. "4 Reasons Why Crumbs Bake Shop Massively Failed." *Business Insider*, July 8, 2014. https://www.businessinsider.com/4-reasons-why-crumbs-bake-shop-closed-2014-7.

11. Dweck, Carol. "Transcript of 'The Power of Believing That You Can Improve.'" TED, November 2014. https://www.ted.com/talks/carol_dweck_the_power_of_believing_that_you_can_improve/transcript?language=en.

12. United States. National Aeronautics and Space Administration. *Report to the President: Actions to Implement the Recommendations of the Presidential Commission on the Space Shuttle Challenger Accident.* Washington, DC: NASA (Supt. of Docs., U.S. G.P.O., distributor), 1986.

13. Ibid.

14. Dunbar, Brian. "Engineer Who Opposed Challenger Launch Offers Personal Look at Tragedy." NASA, accessed June 7, 2020. https://www.nasa.gov/centers/langley/news/researchernews/rn_Colloquium1012.html.

15. United States. National Aeronautics and Space Administration. *Report to the President: Actions to Implement the Recommendations of the Presidential Commission on the Space Shuttle Challenger Accident.* Washington, DC: NASA (Supt. of Docs., U.S. G.P.O., distributor), 1986.

16. "Transcript." NASA, accessed June 7, 2020. https://history.nasa.gov/transcript.html.

17. Pruitt, Sarah. "5 Things You May Not Know about the Challenger Shuttle Disaster." History.com. A&E Television Networks, January 28, 2016. https://www.history.com/news/5-things-you-might-not-know-about-the-challenger-shuttle-disaster.

18. Sierra, Walter. *Beyond the Saga of Rocket Science.* Bloomington, IN: Xlibris, 2019.

19. United States. National Aeronautics and Space Administration. *Report to the President: Actions to Implement the Recommendations of the Presidential Commission on the Space Shuttle Challenger Accident.* Washington, DC: NASA (Supt. of Docs., U.S. G.P.O., distributor), 1986.

20. Ibid., 250.

CHAPTER 2

1. Wikipedia contributors. "Six Sigma," Wikipedia, The Free Encyclopedia, accessed January 31, 2020. https://en.wikipedia.org/w/index.php?title=Six_Sigma&oldid=937045305.

2. Ibid.

3. Galley, Mark. "Problem Solving—3 Basic Steps." Simple Effective Root Cause Analysis Techniques, accessed January 31, 2020. https://blog.thinkreliability.com/problem-solving-three-basic-steps.

4. Ibid.

5. Ibid.

6. "National Geographic Learning and English Language Teaching." National Geographic Learning | English Learning Programs and Resources, accessed January 31, 2020. https://eltngl.com/.

7. "Equifax Data Breach Settlement." Federal Trade Commission, February 20, 2020. https://www.ftc.gov/enforcement/cases-proceedings/refunds/equifax-data-breach-settlement.

8. Morgan, Blake. "10 Major Corporate Blunders That Wouldn't Have Happened If Companies Listened to Their Employees." *Forbes Magazine*, January 4, 2018. https://www.forbes.com/sites/blakemorgan/2018/01/03/10-major-corporate-blunders-that-wouldnt-have-happened-if-companies-listened-to-their-employees/.

9. That's exactly what happened to Wells Fargo customers nationwide. "5,300 Wells Fargo Employees Fired over 2 Million Phony Accounts." CNN Money. Cable News Network, accessed June 7, 2020. https://money.cnn.com/2016/09/08/investing/wells-fargo-created-phony-accounts-bank-fees/index.html.

10. Morgan, Blake. "10 Major Corporate Blunders That Wouldn't Have Happened If Companies Listened to Their Employees." *Forbes Magazine*, January 4, 2018. https://www.forbes.com/sites/blakemorgan/2018/01/03/10-major-corporate-blunders-that-wouldnt-have-happened-if-companies-listened-to-their-employees/.

11. Moynihan, Tim. "Samsung Finally Reveals Why the Note 7 Kept Exploding." *Wired*, June 3, 2017. https://www.wired.com/2017/01/why-the-samsung-galaxy-note-7-kept-exploding/.

12. Morgan, Blake. "10 Major Corporate Blunders That Wouldn't Have Happened If Companies Listened to Their Employees." *Forbes Magazine*, January 4, 2018. https://www.forbes.com/sites/blakemorgan/2018/01/03/10-major-corporate-blunders-that-wouldnt-have-happened-if-companies-listened-to-their-employees/.

13. Survivor. 1982. "Eye of the Tiger." Track 1. Scotti Brothers Records, album.

CHAPTER 3

1. Keith, Patt. "Tips to Improve Problem-Solving Skills and Reduce Stress." UPMC & Pitt Health Sciences News Blog. UPMC, January 19, 2017. https://inside.upmc.com/problem-solving-skills-reduce-stress/.

2. "IS-101.C: Preparing for Federal Disaster Operations: FEMA." Federal Emergency Management Agency | Emergency Management Institute, accessed February 8, 2020. https://training.fema.gov/is/courseoverview.aspx?code=IS-101.c.

3. "IS-100.C: Introduction to the Incident Command System, ICS 100." Federal Emergency Management Agency | Emergency Management Institute, accessed February 8, 2020. https://training.fema.gov/is/courseoverview.aspx?code=IS-100.c.

4. Chalasani, Radhika. "35th Anniversary of the End of the U.S. Hostage Crisis in Iran." CBS News. CBS Interactive, January 20, 2016. https://www.cbsnews.com/pictures/look-back-u-s-hostage-crisis-iran-1979/.

5. Ibid.

6. CBSNews.com. "Reagan's Lucky Day." CBS News, accessed February 2, 2020. https://web.archive.org/web/20130515223652/http://www.cbsnews.com/stories/2001/01/19/iran/main265499.shtml.

7. Blakemore, Erin. "U.S.-Iran Tensions: From Political Coup to Hostage Crisis to Drone Strikes." History.com. A&E Television Networks, May 8, 2018. https://www.history.com/news/iran-nuclear-deal-sanctions-facts-hostage-crisis.

8. *Argo*, directed by Ben Affleck. Telluride, Colorado. Warner Bros. Pictures, 2012.

9. Ibid.

10. Mendez, Antonio, and Matt Baglio. "The True Story behind Operation 'Argo' to Rescue Americans from Iran." The Daily Beast, September 17, 2012. https://www.the dailybeast.com/the-true-story-behind-operation-argo-to-rescue-americans-from-iran.

11. "Rescue of the 'Canadian Six'—a Classic Case of Deception." Central Intelligence Agency, November 21, 2012. https://www.cia.gov/about-cia/cia-museum/experience-the-collection/text-version/stories/rescue-of-the-canadian-six-a-classic-case-of-deception.html.

12. Hewitt, Kate, and Richard Nephew. "How the Iran Hostage Crisis Shaped the US Approach to Sanctions." Brookings, March 12, 2019. https://www.brookings.edu/blog/order-from-chaos/2019/03/12/how-the-iran-hostage-crisis-shaped-the-us-approach-to-sanctions/.

13. Kloefkorn, Sheila. "How to Develop a Problem Solving Culture in Your Company." LinkedIn, April 7, 2016, accessed February 8, 2020. https://www.linkedin.com/pulse/how-develop-problem-solving-culture-your-company-sheila-kloefkorn/.

14. Ibid.

15. Bowden, Adley. "The Supply & Demand Economics behind the Current VC Boom and Crunch." PitchBook, February 22, 2016. https://pitchbook.com/news/articles/the-supply-demand-economics-behind-the-current-vc-boom-and-crunch.

16. Gartenstein, Devra. "Why Is Financial Management So Important in Business?" Your Business, April 5, 2018. https://yourbusiness.azcentral.com/financial-management-important-business-4406.html.

17. Smith, Alasdair, Priyanshu Patwa, and Seguya. "5 Factors That Influence Business Environment." Paypervids, August 18, 2019. https://www.paypervids.com/factors-influence-business-environment/.

18. Uzialko, Adam C. "How Regulatory Changes Could Affect Your Business This Year." Business News Daily. businessnewsdaily.com, July 9, 2018. https://www.businessnewsdaily.com/7671-regulatory-issues-changes.html.

19. Mind Tools Content Team. "Team Building Exercises and Activities: Making Team Building an Everyday Priority." Training from MindTools.com, accessed June 13, 2020. https://www.mindtools.com/pages/article/newTMM_52.htm.

20. Ibid.

21. Ibid.

22. Herman, Zach. "National Employment Monthly Update," accessed June 14, 2020. https://www.ncsl.org/research/labor-and-employment/national-employment-monthly-update.aspx.

23. Ibid.

CHAPTER 4

1. "Reason." Merriam-Webster, accessed April 23, 2020. https://www.merriam-webster.com/dictionary/reason.

2. Ibid.

3. "Publilius Syrus Quotes." BrainyQuote. Xplore, accessed April 23, 2020. https://www.brainyquote.com/quotes/publilius_syrus_136056.

4. "Career Guide." Jobs, accessed April 23, 2020. https://www.indeed.com/career-advice/career-development/strengthen-logical-thinking-skills.

5. "How Does Summit Senior High School Rank among America's Best High Schools?" U.S. News & World Report, accessed April 26, 2020. https://www.usnews.com/education/best-high-schools/new-jersey/districts/summit-public-schools/summit-senior-high-school-12773.

CHAPTER 5

1. "The More You Know TV Commercials." iSpot.tv. Accessed April 26, 2020. https://www.ispot.tv/brands/d93/the-more-you-know.

2. "What Is STEAM Education?" The Institute for Arts Integration and STEAM. Accessed January 14, 2020. https://educationcloset.com/what-is-steam-education-in-k-12-schools/.

3. Harris, William. "How the Scientific Method Works." HowStuffWorks Science. January 27, 2020. https://science.howstuffworks.com/innovation/scientific-experiments/scientific-method3.htm.

4. Wikipedia contributors, "Francis Bacon," Wikipedia, The Free Encyclopedia. Accessed April 26, 2020. https://en.wikipedia.org/w/index.php?title=Francis_Bacon&oldid=950874109.

5. Ibid.

6. Wikipedia contributors, "Scientific method," Wikipedia, The Free Encyclopedia. Accessed April 26, 2020. https://en.wikipedia.org/w/index.php?title=Scientific_method&oldid=952581714.

7. Willson, Amelia. "The Top 5 Free Survey Makers." Search Engine Journal. Accessed July 29, 2019. https://www.searchenginejournal.com/top-5-free-survey-makers/318003/#close.

8. Ibid.

9. "General Problem-Solving Steps." ETS. Accessed April 26, 2020. https://www.ets.org/gre/revised_general/prepare/quantitative_reasoning/problem_solving/.

10. "Fulbright's Second Annual Litigation Trends Survey." Accessed April 27, 2020. http://www.fulbright.com/mediaroom/files/fj0536-us-v13.pdf.

11. Ibid.

12. "The Basics: What Is e-Discovery?" Complete Discovery Source. Accessed May 3, 2020. https://cdslegal.com/knowledge/the-basics-what-is-e-discovery/.

13. Al-Attili, A. "Unit 1 Introduction to Research." 2.1 Why research? The role of information. Accessed April 26, 2020. https://www.soas.ac.uk/cedep-demos/000_P506_RM_3736-Demo/unit1/page_15.htm.

CHAPTER 6

1. Heshmat, Shahram. "Why Do We Remember Certain Things, But Forget Others?" *Psychology Today*. Sussex Publishers, October 8, 2015. https://www.psychologytoday.com/us/blog/science-choice/201510/why-do-we-remember-certain-things-forget-others.

2. Jackson, Gabrielle. "Conversation's Last Refuge: The Art, and Heart, of Talking about the Weather | Gabrielle Jackson." *The Guardian*, February 20, 2017. https://

www.theguardian.com/commentisfree/2017/feb/20/conversations-last-refuge-the-art-and-heart-of-talking-about-the-weather.

3. Pheko, Lipholo, and Lipholo Pheko. "It's All about Networking." *The Post*, March 29, 2019. https://www.thepost.co.ls/business/its-all-about-networking/.

4. Ibid.

5. Uzzi, Brian, and Shannon Dunlap. "How to Build Your Network." *Harvard Business Review*, August 1, 2014. https://hbr.org/2005/12/how-to-build-your-network.

6. Gladwell, Malcolm. *The Tipping Point: How Little Things Can Make a Big Difference*. Rockland, MA: Wheeler, 2003.

7. Klein, Christopher. "The Midnight Ride of William Dawes." History.com. A&E Television Networks, April 18, 2012. https://www.history.com/news/the-midnight-ride-of-william-dawes.

CHAPTER 7

1. Oster, Erik D. "AT&T Shows What's Wrong with Settling for Just an 'OK' Network." Adweek, January 2, 2019. https://www.adweek.com/brand-marketing/att-shows-whats-wrong-with-settling-for-just-an-ok-network/.

2. "About Us." Glassdoor About Us, accessed May 21, 2020. https://www.glassdoor.com/about-us/.

3. Sinek, Simon. *Start with Why: How Great Leaders Inspire Everyone to Take Action*. London: Portfolio Penguin, 2019.

4. Collins, James C. *Good to Great*. London: Random House Business, 2001.

5. Liman, Doug, Patrick Timothy Crowley, Richard N. Gladstein, Tony Gilroy, William Blake Herron, Matt Damon, Franka Potente, et al. 2008. *The Bourne Identity*. Universal City, CA: Universal Studios Home Entertainment.

CHAPTER 8

1. "Communicate." Merriam-Webster, accessed February 27, 2020. https://www.merriam-webster.com/dictionary/communicate.

2. Weekley, Ernest. *An Etymological Dictionary of Modern English: With a New Biographical Memoir of the Author by Montague Weekley*. New York: Dover, 1967, p. 338.

3. "Watch Live or Archived TVW Events." TVW Washington States Public Affairs Network, accessed April 13, 2020. https://www.tvw.org/watch/?eventID=2020031146; staff, CalMatters. "Timeline: California Reacts to Coronavirus." CalMatters, April 8, 2020. https://calmatters.org/health/coronavirus/2020/04/gavin-newsom-coronavirus-updates-timeline/#First case of COVID-19 in California; "ICYMI: Governor Ron DeSantis' Live Stream Regarding COVID-19." Florida Governor Ron DeSantis, accessed April 13, 2020. https://www.flgov.com/2020/03/23/icymi-governor-ron-desantis-live-stream-regarding-covid-19/.

4. "Coronavirus." World Health Organization, accessed April 13, 2020. https://www.who.int/emergencies/diseases/novel-coronavirus-2019.

5. ABC News, accessed April 13, 2020. https://abcnews.go.com/US/timeline-cuomos-trumps-responses-coronavirus-outbreak/story?id=69914641.

6. Facher, Lev, Jim Gilbert, et al. "Who's Who, among the Trump Administration's Coronavirus Response Team." STAT, April 2, 2020. https://www.statnews.com/2020/03/20/guide-to-trump-administration-coronavirus-response-team/.

7. Ibid.

8. Jelinek, David. "Why Smart People Surround Themselves with Smarter People." SUCCESS, July 19, 2016. https://www.success.com/why-smart-people-surround-themselves-with-smarter-people/.

9. Ibid.

10. Rahm Emanuel Quotes. BrainyQuote.com, Brainy Media Inc., 2020. https://www.brainyquote.com/quotes/rahm_emanuel_409199, accessed April 14, 2020.

11. A Guide for Manufacturers, Importers, Distributors and Retailers on Reporting under Sections 15 and 37 of the Consumer Product Safety Act and Section 102 of the Child Safety Protection Act and Preparing for, Initiating, and Implementing Product Safety Recalls § (2012), p. 2.

12. Fleming, Sean. "Almost All Businesses Expect to Face a Crisis. And How They Deal with Them Really Counts." World Economic Forum, August 6, 2019. https://www.weforum.org/agenda/2019/08/business-leader-corporate-crisis/.

13. "About Coronavirus Disease 2019 (COVID-19)." Centers for Disease Control and Prevention, February 24, 2020. https://www.cdc.gov/coronavirus/2019-ncov/about/index.html.

14. Tyler, Clifford. "Web Traffic Spiked 20% in One Week amid Coronavirus Shutdown, Verizon CEO Says." CNBC, March 20, 2020. https://www.cnbc.com/2020/03/19/verizon-ceo-web-traffic-up-20percent-in-one-week-amid-coronavirus-shutdown.html.

15. Ibid.

16. More States Extend School Closures—School Business Daily SBDaily@asbo.emm.us.com—March 24, 2020. "Idaho Board of Education Orders Schools Closed Statewide." U.S. News & World Report, accessed March 24, 2020. https://www.usnews.com/news/best-states/idaho/articles/2020-03-23/more-than-5-dozen-idaho-residents-confirmed-to-have-covid-19; Waldrop, Theresa. "More States Extend School Closures, Some through the End of the School Year." CNN. Cable News Network, March 23, 2020. https://edition.cnn.com/2020/03/23/us/us-schools-extend-closing-coronavirus/index.html.

17. "Influencer Marketing Benchmark Report: 2019." Influencer Marketing Hub, 2019. https://influencermarketinghub.com/IM_Benchmark_Report_2019.pdf.

18. Ibid.

19. "What Is Influencer Marketing?: Read the Ultimate Guide." TapInfluence, November 13, 2019. https://www.tapinfluence.com/blog-what-is-influencer-marketing/#what_is.

CHAPTER 9

1. Deutsch, David. *The Beginning of Infinity: Explanations That Transform the World.* London: Penguin, 2011.

2. "Lives of the Prophets." Lives of the Prophets—New World Encyclopedia, accessed May 9, 2020. https://www.newworldencyclopedia.org/entry/Lives_of_the_Prophets.

3. Lung, Han-Gwon. "3 CEOs That Saved Their Companies by Making Unpopular Decisions." *Business Insider*, October 10, 2016. https://www.businessinsider.com/ceos-that-saved-their-companies-by-making-unpopular-decisions-2016-10.

4. Ibid.

5. Ibid.

6. "Chicago Tylenol Murders." Crime Museum, accessed May 9, 2020. https://www.crimemuseum.org/crime-library/cold-cases/chicago-tylenol-murders/.

7. Lung, Han-Gwon. "3 CEOs That Saved Their Companies by Making Unpopular Decisions." *Business Insider*, October 10, 2016. https://www.businessinsider.com/ceos-that-saved-their-companies-by-making-unpopular-decisions-2016-10.

8. Ibid.

9. Pepe, Louis. Interview with Henry Johnson, Former Packaging Supervisor, Merck & Co (MRK.N) and Schering-Plough Corp (SGP.N.) Personal Interview, May 10, 2020.

10. Knowledge@Wharton. "Tylenol and the Legacy of J&J's James Burke." *Time*, October 5, 2012. https://business.time.com/2012/10/05/tylenol-and-the-legacy-of-jjs-james-burke/.

11. Bareilles, Sara, and Jack Antonoff. "The Blessed Unrest." Track 1. Epic Records, compact disc, 2013.

12. BRAVE 2012—Pixar, Walt Disney Pictures. Directors: Mark Andrews, Brenda Chapman (codirector), Steve Purcell (codirector); Producer: Katherine Sarafian, accessed May 9, 2020.

13. Wikipedia contributors, "Herb Brooks," Wikipedia, The Free Encyclopedia, accessed June 12, 2020. https://en.wikipedia.org/w/index.php?title=Herb_Brooks&oldid=958664902.

14. Walt Disney Pictures presents a Mayhem Pictures production; produced by Mark Ciardi and Gordon Gray; written by Eric Guggenheim; directed by Gavin O'Connor. *Miracle*. (Burbank, CA): Walt Disney Home Entertainment: Buena Vista Home Entertainment, 2004.

15. Bareilles, Sara, and Jack Antonoff. "The Blessed Unrest." Track 1. Epic Records, compact disc, 2013.

CHAPTER 10

1. Quartz. Twitter Post. May 18, 2020, 10:36 AM. https://twitter.com/qz/status/1262391711130619905/photo/1.

2. "What Is Problem Solving and Why Is It Important." Kepner, accessed May 24, 2020. https://www.kepner-tregoe.com/blog/what-is-problem-solving-and-why-is-it-important/.

3. Wikipedia contributors, "Francis Bacon," Wikipedia, The Free Encyclopedia, accessed April 26, 2020. https://en.wikipedia.org/w/index.php?title=Francis_Bacon&oldid=950874109.

4. Suciu, Peter. "More Americans Are Getting Their News from Social Media." *Forbes Magazine*, October 11, 2019. https://www.forbes.com/sites/petersuciu/2019/10/11/more-americans-are-getting-their-news-from-social-media/ (accessed May 22, 2020).

5. Guss, Stephen. "How Do CEOs Consume Content? Quartz Asked 940 Executives to Find Out." brandchannel, July 21, 2015. https://www.brandchannel.com/2015/07/21/ceos-consume-content-072115/ (accessed May 20, 2020).

6. Exec. Order. No. 104, NJ (March 16, 2020), https://www.nj.gov/infobank/eo/056murphy/pdf/EO-104.pdf.

7. Exec. Order. No. 107, NJ (March 21, 2020), https://www.nj.gov/infobank/eo/056murphy/pdf/EO-107.pdf.

8. Muccari, Robin, Denise Chow, and Joe Murphy. "Coronavirus Timeline: Tracking the Critical Moments of COVID-19." NBCNews.com. NBC Universal News Group, May 11, 2020. https://www.nbcnews.com/health/health-news/coronavirus-timeline-tracking-critical-moments-covid-19-n1154341.

9. Ibid.

10. Ibid.

11. Ibid.

12. Wikipedia contributors, "William James," Wikipedia, The Free Encyclopedia, accessed May 29, 2020. https://en.wikipedia.org/w/index.php?title=William_James&oldid=957023277.

13. Stottler, Wayne. "What Is Problem Solving and Why Is It Important." Kepner, accessed May 30, 2020. https://www.kepner-tregoe.com/blog/what-is-problem-solving-and-why-is-it-important/.

References

Al-Attili, A. "Unit 1 Introduction to Research: 2.1 Why Research? The Role of Information." May 3, 2020. https://www.soas.ac.uk/cedep-demos/000_P506_RM_3736-Demo/unit1/page_15.htm.

Blakemore, Erin. "U.S.-Iran Tensions: From Political Coup to Hostage Crisis to Drone Strikes." History.com. A&E Television Networks, May 8, 2018. https://www.history.com/news/iran-nuclear-deal-sanctions-facts-hostage-crisis.

Bowden, Adley. "The Supply & Demand Economics behind the Current VC Boom and Crunch." PitchBook, February 22, 2016. https://pitchbook.com/news/articles/the-supply-demand-economics-behind-the-current-vc-boom-and-crunch.

Chalasani, Radhika. "35th Anniversary of the End of the U.S. Hostage Crisis in Iran." CBS News, January 20, 2016. https://www.cbsnews.com/pictures/look-back-u-s-hostage-crisis-iran-1979/.

Collins, James C. *Good to Great.* London: Random House Business, 2001.

DeMers, Jayson. "5 Companies That Grew Too Quickly (and What You Can Learn from Them)." Entrepreneur, March 12, 2018. https://www.entrepreneur.com/article/310166.

Deutsch, David. *The Beginning of Infinity: Explanations That Transform the World.* London: Penguin, 2011.

Dunbar, Brian. "Engineer Who Opposed Challenger Launch Offers Personal Look at Tragedy." NASA. June 7, 2020. https://www.nasa.gov/centers/langley/news/researchernews/rn_Colloquium1012.html.

Dweck, Carol. "What Having a 'Growth Mindset' Actually Means." *Harvard Business Review*, January 13, 2016. https://hbr.org/2016/01/what-having-a-growth-mindset-actually-means.

Facher, Lev, Jim Gilbert, et al. "Who's Who, among the Trump Administration's Coronavirus Response Team." STAT, April 2, 2020. https://www.statnews.com/2020/03/20/guide-to-trump-administration-coronavirus-response-team/.

Fleming, Sean. "Almost All Businesses Expect to Face a Crisis. And How They Deal with Them Really Counts." World Economic Forum, August 6, 2019. https://www.weforum.org/agenda/2019/08/business-leader-corporate-crisis/.

Friedman, Thomas L. "How to Get a Job at Google." *New York Times*, February 22, 2014. https://www.nytimes.com/2014/02/23/opinion/sunday/friedman-how-to-get-a-job-at-google.html.

Galley, Mark. "Problem Solving—3 Basic Steps." Simple Effective Root Cause Analysis Techniques. January 31, 2020. https://blog.thinkreliability.com/problem-solving-three-basic-steps.

Gartenstein, Devra. "Why Is Financial Management So Important in Business?" Your Business, April 5, 2018. https://yourbusiness.azcentral.com/financial-management-important-business-4406.html.

Gladwell, Malcolm. *The Tipping Point: How Little Things Can Make a Big Difference*. Rockland, MA: Wheeler, 2003.

Guss, Stephen. "How Do CEOs Consume Content? Quartz Asked 940 Executives to Find Out." brandchannel, July 21, 2015. https://www.brandchannel.com/2015/07/21/ceos-consume-content-072115/.

Harris, William. "How the Scientific Method Works." HowStuffWorks Science, January 27, 2020. https://science.howstuffworks.com/innovation/scientific-experiments/scientific-method3.htm.

Herman, Zach. "National Employment Monthly Update." June 14, 2020. https://www.ncsl.org/research/labor-and-employment/national-employment-monthly-update.aspx.

Heshmat, Shahram. "Why Do We Remember Certain Things, But Forget Others?" *Psychology Today*. Sussex Publishers, October 8, 2015. https://www.psychologytoday.com/us/blog/science-choice/201510/why-do-we-remember-certain-things-forget-others.

Hewitt, Kate, and Richard Nephew. "How the Iran Hostage Crisis Shaped the US Approach to Sanctions." Brookings, March 12, 2019. https://www.brookings.edu/blog/order-from-chaos/2019/03/12/how-the-iran-hostage-crisis-shaped-the-us-approach-to-sanctions/.

Jackson, Gabrielle. "Conversation's Last Refuge: The Art, and Heart, of Talking about the Weather | Gabrielle Jackson." *The Guardian*, February 20, 2017. https://www.theguardian.com/commentisfree/2017/feb/20/conversations-last-refuge-the-art-and-heart-of-talking-about-the-weather.

Jelinek, David. "Why Smart People Surround Themselves with Smarter People." SUCCESS, July 19, 2016. https://www.success.com/why-smart-people-surround-themselves-with-smarter-people/.

Klein, Christopher. "The Midnight Ride of William Dawes." History.com. A&E Television Networks, April 18, 2012. https://www.history.com/news/the-midnight-ride-of-william-dawes.

Kloefkorn, Sheila. "How to Develop a Problem Solving Culture in Your Company." LinkedIn, April 7, 2016. https://www.linkedin.com/pulse/how-develop-problem-solving-culture-your-company-sheila-kloefkorn/.

Liman, Doug, Patrick Timothy Crowley, Richard N. Gladstein, Tony Gilroy, William Blake Herron, Matt Damon, Franka Potente, et al. *The Bourne Identity*. Universal City, CA: Universal Studios Home Entertainment, 2008.

Lung, Han-Gwon. "3 CEOs That Saved Their Companies by Making Unpopular Decisions." Business Insider, October 10, 2016. https://www.businessinsider.com/ceos-that-saved-their-companies-by-making-unpopular-decisions-2016-10.

Mendez, Antonio, and Matt Baglio. "The True Story behind Operation 'Argo' to Rescue Americans from Iran." *The Daily Beast*, September 17, 2012. https://www.thedaily beast.com/the-true-story-behind-operation-argo-to-rescue-americans-from-iran.

Morgan, Blake. "10 Major Corporate Blunders That Wouldn't Have Happened If Companies Listened to Their Employees." *Forbes Magazine*, January 4, 2018. https://www.forbes.com/sites/blakemorgan/2018/01/03/10-major-corporate-blun ders-that-wouldnt-have-happened-if-companies-listened-to-their-employees/.

Moynihan, Tim. "Samsung Finally Reveals Why the Note 7 Kept Exploding." *Wired*, June 3, 2017. https://www.wired.com/2017/01/why-the-samsung-galaxy-note-7-kept-exploding/.

Muccari, Robin, Denise Chow, and Joe Murphy. "Coronavirus Timeline: Tracking the Critical Moments of COVID-19." NBC News.com, May 11, 2020. https://www.nbcnews.com/health/health-news/coronavirus-timeline-tracking-critical-moments-covid-19-n1154341.

Oster, Erik D. "AT&T Shows What's Wrong with Settling for Just an 'OK' Network." *Adweek*, January 2, 2019. https://www.adweek.com/brand-marketing/att-shows-whats-wrong-with-settling-for-just-an-ok-network/.

Patt, Keith. "Tips to Improve Problem-Solving Skills and Reduce Stress." UPMC & Pitt Health Sciences News Blog, January 19, 2017. https://inside.upmc.com/problem-solving-skills-reduce-stress/.

Peterson, Hayley. "4 Reasons Why Crumbs Bake Shop Massively Failed." *Business Insider*, July 8, 2014. https://www.businessinsider.com/4-reasons-why-crumbs-bake-shop-closed-2014-7.

Pheko, Lipholo. "It's All about Networking." *The Post*, March 29, 2019. https://www.thepost.co.ls/business/its-all-about-networking/.

Pruitt, Sarah. "5 Things You May Not Know about the Challenger Shuttle Disaster." History.com. A&E Television Networks, January 28, 2016. https://www.history.com/news/5-things-you-might-not-know-about-the-challenger-shuttle-disaster.

Randazzo, Sara. "Crumbs Bake Shop Closing Its Doors." *Wall Street Journal*, July 8, 2014. https://www.wsj.com/articles/sticky-time-for-crumbs-bake-shop-1404770884.

Sierra, Walter. *Beyond the Saga of Rocket Science*. Bloomington, IN: Xlibris, 2019.

Sinek, Simon. *Start with Why: How Great Leaders Inspire Everyone to Take Action*. London: Portfolio Penguin, 2019.

Smith, Alasdair, Priyanshu Patwa, and Seguya. "5 Factors That Influence Business Environment." Paypervids, August 18, 2019. https://www.paypervids.com/factors-influence-business-environment/.

Stottler, Wayne. "What Is Problem Solving and Why Is It Important." Kepner. May 30, 2020. https://www.kepner-tregoe.com/blog/what-is-problem-solving-and-why-is-it-important/.

Suciu, Peter. "More Americans Are Getting Their News from Social Media." *Forbes Magazine*, October 11, 2019. https://www.forbes.com/sites/petersuciu/2019/10/11/more-americans-are-getting-their-news-from-social-media/.

Sundem, Garth. *Beyond IQ: Scientific Tools for Training Problem Solving, Intuition, Emotional Intelligence, Creativity, and More*. New York: Three Rivers Press, 2014.

Tyler, Clifford. "Web Traffic Spiked 20% in One Week amid Coronavirus Shutdown, Verizon CEO Says." CNBC, March 20, 2020. https://www.cnbc.com/2020/03/19/

verizon-ceo-web-traffic-up-20percent-in-one-week-amid-coronavirus-shutdown. html.

Uzialko, Adam C. "How Regulatory Changes Could Affect Your Business This Year." *Business News Daily*, July 9, 2018. https://www.businessnewsdaily.com/7671-regulatory-issues-changes.html.

Uzzi, Brian, and Shannon Dunlap. "How to Build Your Network." *Harvard Business Review*, August 1, 2014. https://hbr.org/2005/12/how-to-build-your-network.

Waldrop, Theresa. "More States Extend School Closures, Some through the End of the School Year." CNN, March 23, 2020. https://edition.cnn.com/2020/03/23/us/us-schools-extend-closing-coronavirus/index.html.

Weekley, Ernest. *An Etymological Dictionary of Modern English: With a New Biographical Memoir of the Author by Montague Weekley*. New York: Dover, 1967, p. 338.

Willson, Amelia. "The Top 5 Free Survey Makers." *Search Engine Journal*, July 29, 2019. https://www.searchenginejournal.com/top-5-free-survey-makers/318003/#close.

About the Author

Louis J. Pepe is the author of *Smarter Decision Making—Avoiding Poor Decisions Effective Listening*, the first in the RBL series on leadership.

He is assistant superintendent/CFO for the City of Summit Public Schools in Union County, New Jersey. He has more than thirty years of leadership experience between military, private, and public service focused on leadership, management, operations, and administration.

Lou is a speaker, mentor, and adjunct professor at Montclair State University. His knowledge and success has positioned him as a go-to resource for other professionals throughout the industry. A member of the Oxford Roundtable, Lou presented on Issues in Financing Public Education in America at Oxford University in Oxford, England, in 2005.

He is president and owner of Lou Pepe Presentations, LLC, consulting on effective management strategies and leadership training through presentations designed for workshops, seminars, conferences, and business meetings.

As a keynote speaker and presenter, Lou has engaged audiences across the country with his down-to-earth, practical advice and insights into today's challenges in managing people and situations to accomplish organizational goals and objectives.

His blog http://businessedissues.blogspot.com/ has gained readership from countries all over the world and featured as "best of blogs" by the American Association of School Administrators.

HONORS AND AWARDS

- School Business Administrator of the Year—New Jersey Association of School Business Officials 2018

- Distinguished Service Award—New Jersey Association of School Business Officials 2018
- Eagle Award 2015 ASBO—Association of School Business Officials International Leadership Achievement Awards
- Pinnacle of Achievement for Innovative Ideas in the field of School Business 2007 ASBO—Association of School Business Officials International
- Oxford Roundtable—2005—Speaker on Issues in Financing Public Education in America, Oxford University, Oxford, England
- Recipient of the U.S. Army Commendation Medal (ARCOM) oak leaf cluster and Achievement Medal

EDUCATION

Mr. Pepe earned his bachelor's degree in international business and business administration from Ramapo College of New Jersey and an MBA in finance from William Paterson University's Christos M. Cotsakos College of Business.

BACKGROUND

Prior to entering the field of education, Mr. Pepe was a scanning administrator for the Atlantic & Pacific Tea Company, administrative assistant for SL Industries, and served in the U.S. Army Signal Corps as a tactical signal operator 72E, in Darmstadt, Germany, USAISC as MARS Radio operator at Fort Campbell, Kentucky, and as an Automated Telecommunications Specialist 72G Shift Supervisor with the 66th Military Intelligence Brigade, Munich, Germany. Through these experiences, Mr. Pepe developed leadership skills in team building, management, and communications.

He is currently a past president of New Jersey Association of School Business Officials, served two terms as a Councilman at Large in his home community, and continues to serve as a mentor for NJ Dept. of Education State Certification Program. Lou is on faculty at Montclair State University as an adjunct professor in the Graduate Program in Education.

He and his wife live in Lincoln Park, New Jersey, and have two daughters and three grandchildren.

www.ingramcontent.com/pod-product-compliance
Lightning Source LLC
Chambersburg PA
CBHW021602210326
41599CB00010B/567